Cooking Light®

5 Ingredient
15 MINUTE
COOKBOOK

Cooking Light® 5-Ingredient 15-Minute Cookbook
©1999 by Oxmoor House, Inc.
Book Division of Southern Progress Corporation
P.O. Box 2463, Birmingham, AL 35201

Library of Congress Catalog Number: 99-70264
ISBN: 0-8487-1852-6
Manufactured in the United States of America
First Printing 1999

Be sure to check with your health-care provider before making any
changes in your diet.

Editor-in-Chief: Nancy Fitzpatrick Wyatt
Senior Foods Editor: Katherine M. Eakin
Senior Editor, Copy and Homes: Olivia Kindig Wells
Art Director: James Boone

5-Ingredient 15-Minute Cookbook
Editor: Anne Chappell Cain, M.S., M.P.H., R.D.
Copy Editor: Jacqueline Giovanelli
Editorial Assistant: Heather Averett
Designer: Carol O. Loria
Director, Test Kitchens: Kathleen Royal Phillips
Assistant Director, Test Kitchens: Gayle Hays Sadler
Test Kitchens Staff: Julie Christopher, Natalie E. King, Laurie Victoria Knowles,
    Carolyn Land, Regan Miller, Jan A. Smith, Kate Wheeler, R.D.
Contributing Recipe Developers: Karen Levin, Elizabeth Luckett, Carol H. Munson,
    OTT Communications, Elizabeth Taliaferro, Lisa H. Talley
Senior Photographer: Jim Bathie
Photographer: Brit Huckabay
Senior Photo Stylist: Kay Clarke
Photo Stylist: Virginia R. Cravens
Publishing Systems Administrator: Rick Tucker
Production and Distribution Director: Phillip Lee
Associate Production Manager: Theresa L. Beste
Associate Production Manager: James McDaniel
Production Assistant: Faye Porter Bonner

We're Here for You!
We at Oxmoor House are dedicated to serving you with reliable
information that expands your imagination and enriches your life.
We welcome your comments and suggestions.
Please write to us at:

Oxmoor House, Inc.
Editor, *5-Ingredient 15-Minute Cookbook*
2100 Lakeshore Drive
Birmingham, AL 35209

To order additional copies of this publication or any others, call 1-205-877-6560.

Cover: Beef Stir-Fry with Oyster Sauce, page 97

Skillet Ziti and Vegetables, page 66

contents

75% of Americans don't know at 4 p.m. what they'll eat for dinner, but whatever it is had better be healthy, tasty, and fast.

Introduction

With the *5-Ingredient 15-Minute Cookbook,* we've achieved all three criteria and created a cookbook that will help you take some of the guesswork out of meal planning. Now you can

- simplify your grocery shopping,

- spend less time in the kitchen, and

- satisfy your soul and body with delicious, wholesome meals.

7 Suppertime Solutions

While this book can't add minutes to your day, it can help get you in and out of the kitchen quickly and still give you the satisfaction of serving your family healthy meals.

We started with the basic questions: **What am I going to cook? Do I have the ingredients or do I need to go to the store? How long will it take? Will the meal satisfy my family?** We've given you the answers with 94 quick meals that your family will enjoy. With each turn of the page, you'll find a meal that fits into your busy schedule: a 5-ingredient meal; a 15-minute meal; or a 5-ingredient *and* 15-minute meal.

1 Will I Need to Go to the Grocery Store?

Maybe not. Many of the recipes use the same pantry and frozen ingredients so that you can stock up and always have food items on hand to throw together a meal.

With every meal, you get a grocery list of what you'll need for the whole meal, including salads, side dishes, bread (see **Supermarket Bread Basket** on page 10), and even quick desserts. And the **No-Stress Shopping List** (page 11) helps you stock up on the basic ingredients needed for many of the meals in this book.

2 How Many Ingredients Will It Take?

Usually 5, but never more than 10, not including salt, pepper, water, and cooking spray.

Vegetable Panini with Feta, page 168

3 How Long Will It Take to Make the Recipe?

Never more than 15 minutes of work time. We give you either **work time** and **cook time** or **total time.** Total time is given when there's no down time—it's the time it takes to complete the recipe from start to finish.

When the preparation and the cooking are two distinct steps, we give you the work time and the cook time. The work time is never more than 15 minutes, but there may be some nonactive cook time during which you can be doing something else.

4 What Else Do I Serve?

Instead of just giving you recipe chapters, we're giving you meals. Each meal features a main dish (along with a photograph) and either a short recipe or suggestions for commercial products to round out the meal. The blurb on each page helps you pull the meal all together.

5 But Is It Good for My Family?

It's healthy. Each recipe has the nutrient information for one serving, plus exchange values. Meals contain no more than 30% calories from fat, according to the current dietary recommendations. We suggest a variety of fresh fruits and vegetables, whole grain breads, and low-fat dairy products—all in an effort to take the guesswork out of healthy eating. (For more information, see the **Nutrition Notes** on page 228.)

6 How Else Can I Save Time?

For another timesaving approach, see the **Slow Cooker Suppers** chapter beginning on page 193. For quick-fix accompaniments, the **Mix & Match Recipes** chapter (page 213) shows you how to create fabulous salads and desserts from combinations of only 5 ingredients.

7 What Are You Waiting For?

Starting on page 13, you have 94 meals to work with. That's enough for three months, or one-fourth of the year!

Supermarket Bread Basket

Look no further than the grocery deli or the frozen and refrigerated sections of the supermarket for wonderful breads to serve with your meals.

BREADSTICKS, CRACKERS & CHIPS

From lower left: refrigerated breadsticks, refrigerated corn twists, hard breadsticks, low-fat potato chips, rice cakes, mini rice cakes, low-fat crackers, low-fat tortilla chips

Quick and easy breadstick recipes: Garlic-Cheese Breadsticks (page 141) and Pretzel Breadsticks (page 159)

ROLLS, ROUNDS & LOAVES

From lower left: white, poppy seed rolls, wheatberry, whole wheat, pumpernickel, pumpernickel rolls, Italian, raisin, poppy seed, sun-dried tomato, French, pesto, French rolls, whole wheat rolls, rye, multigrain rolls, mini potato rolls, spinach-feta, sourdough, olive

Quick and easy bread recipes: Garlic Bread (page 39) and Parmesan Toasts (page 85)

FLAT BREADS

From lower left: pita chips, pita bread rounds, flour tortillas, small Boboli crusts, focaccia rounds, large Boboli crusts

Quick and easy chip recipes: Tortilla Wedges (page 57) and Baked Pita Wedges (page 62)

No-Stress Shopping List

If you keep these ingredients on hand, you'll be able to make one-third of the recipes in this book. Use this list to stock up on the basics for quick and easy cooking. Then you won't have to stop at the grocery store and wonder what in the world you can cook for dinner.

Produce
Lemons
Onions
Peppers (green, red)
Potatoes
Salad greens, pre-cut
Spinach
Tomatoes
Zucchini

Breads
Boboli crusts
French bread
Hoagie rolls
Italian bread
Pita bread rounds
Refrigerated pizza crust dough
Tortillas, flour (fat-free)

Canned
(reduced-sodium, low-fat)
Beans (black, kidney, pinto, refried)
Beef broth
Chicken broth
Clams
Cream of chicken soup
Tomato sauce
Tomato soup
Tomatoes: diced, stewed, whole

Grains, Pastas, and Rice
Couscous
Pastas: fettuccine, linguine,
    penne, spaghetti, tortellini, ziti
Rice (boil-in-bag, rice blends)

Dairy
Blue cheese
Cheddar cheese (reduced-fat)
Feta cheese
Mexican cheese (reduced-fat)
Mozzarella cheese, part-skim
Parmesan cheese, shredded
Provolone cheese
Sour cream (fat-free)

Fish, Meats, and Poultry
Beef: deli roast beef, ground
    round, stew meat
Chicken breast halves, skinned
Pork chops
Shrimp, peeled and deveined
Turkey, ground
Turkey sausage

Frozen
Beef strips
Broccoli
Chicken, diced, cooked
Corn
Mixed vegetables
Stir-fry vegetables

Oils/Fats
Cooking sprays
Oils: olive, sesame, vegetable
Reduced-calorie margarine

Condiments
Garlic, minced
Honey
Mustard, Dijon
Olive oil vinaigrette (reduced-fat)
Pasta sauce/spaghetti sauce
Salad dressings (reduced-fat)
Salsa
Soy or teriyaki sauce (low-sodium)
Spreadable fruit, preserves
Vinegar, balsamic
Worcestershire sauce (low-sodium)

Seasonings
Cajun seasoning
Chili powder
Chili seasoning mix
Cinnamon
Cumin
Garlic powder/garlic salt
Garlic-pepper seasoning
Greek seasoning
Italian seasoning
Lemon-herb seasoning
Mexican seasoning
Taco seasoning mix (low-sodium)

Zesty Fettuccine and Shrimp, page 49

56% of AMERICANS spend *less than* 1 hour preparing a weekday meal.

Fish & Shellfish

If you want speedy seafood

- buy peeled and deveined shrimp,

- look for thin pieces of fish (the thinner the fish, the faster it cooks), and

- keep canned fish like tuna, clams, and salmon on hand.

Country Catfish

total time: 14 minutes

Butter-flavored cooking spray
⅔ cup corn flake crumbs
¼ teaspoon salt
¼ teaspoon ground red pepper
4 (4-ounce) farm-raised catfish fillets
2 egg whites, lightly beaten
½ cup corn relish

Line a shallow pan with aluminum foil. Coat with cooking spray.
Combine crumbs, salt, and pepper in a small bowl; stir well. Dip fish in beaten egg whites; dredge in crumb mixture. Place fish in pan. Bake at 450° for 8 to 10 minutes or until fish flakes easily when tested with a fork. Serve immediately with corn relish.
Yield: 4 servings (serving size: 1 fillet and 2 tablespoons relish).

Per Serving: Calories 224 (20% from fat)   Fat 5.0g (sat 1.1g)   Protein 23.6g
Carbohydrate 18.7g   Fiber 0.2g   Cholesterol 66mg   Sodium 429mg
Exchanges: 1 Starch, 3 Lean Meat

· · · · ·

Zesty Coleslaw

total time: 2 minutes

Combine 4 cups coleslaw mix and ⅓ cup fat-free vinaigrette.
Yield: 4 (1-cup) servings.

Per Serving: Calories 27 (3% from fat)   Fat 0.1g (sat 0.0g)   Protein 0.9g
Carbohydrate 6.1g   Fiber 1.7g   Cholesterol 0mg   Sodium 228mg
Exchange: 1 Vegetable

Grocery List

1 (16-ounce) package
coleslaw mix

2 medium-size tomatoes

¼ watermelon

1 jar corn
relish (such as Vidalia)

1 bottle
fat-free vinaigrette

Ground red pepper

1 (21-ounce) box corn
flake crumbs

2 eggs

4 (4-ounce) catfish fillets

Delicious crispy coating! Hard to believe this fish is oven-fried. Serve with Zesty Coleslaw, sliced tomatoes, and watermelon.

Grocery List

3 green onions

1 (6-ounce) package radishes

4 crusty rolls

1 (8-ounce) can crushed pineapple in juice

Dried crushed red pepper

Butter-flavored spray (such as "I Can't Believe It's Not Butter")

Salt-free lemon-herb seasoning (such as Mrs. Dash)

2 (9-ounce) packages frozen Sugar Snap peas

4 (4-ounce) flounder fillets

BROILED FLOUNDER WITH PINEAPPLE SALSA

total time: 12 minutes

4 (4-ounce) flounder fillets
Butter-flavored spray
2 teaspoons salt-free lemon-herb seasoning
¼ teaspoon salt
1 (8-ounce) can crushed pineapple in juice, drained
3 green onions, sliced
⅓ cup chopped radishes
½ teaspoon dried crushed red pepper

Place fish on rack of a broiler pan coated with butter spray. Coat fish with butter spray; sprinkle with lemon-herb seasoning and salt.
Broil fish 5½ inches from heat 8 minutes or until fish flakes easily when tested with a fork.
While fish broils, combine pineapple and remaining ingredients. Top each fillet with ¼ cup pineapple salsa.
Serve immediately.
Yield: 4 servings.

Per Serving: Calories 132 (12% from fat)   Fat 1.7g (sat 0.3g)   Protein 21.7g
Carbohydrate 7.8g   Fiber 0.5g   Cholesterol 54mg   Sodium 243mg
Exchanges: ½ Fruit, 3 Very Lean Meat

Make this pineapple-topped fish a meal

with steamed Sugar Snap peas and crusty rolls.

GROUPER ATHENIAN

total time: 9 minutes

Grocery List

1 plum tomato

Honey

1 (2-ounce) package
sliced almonds

Salt-free Greek seasoning

1 (8-ounce) package
orzo

1 (4-ounce) package
crumbled basil- and
tomato-flavored
feta cheese

1 (10-ounce) package
frozen chopped spinach

½ gallon vanilla low-fat
frozen yogurt

4 (4-ounce) grouper fillets

4   (4-ounce) grouper fillets
2   teaspoons salt-free Greek seasoning
Cooking spray
1   (10-ounce) package frozen chopped spinach, thawed and
      squeezed dry
1   plum tomato, coarsely chopped
¼   cup (1 ounce) crumbled basil- and tomato-flavored feta cheese

Sprinkle both sides of fillets with seasoning. Coat a large nonstick skillet
with cooking spray, and place over medium-high heat until hot. Add
fish, and cook 3 minutes; remove skillet from heat.
Turn fish; top with spinach, tomato, and cheese. Return skillet to heat;
cover and cook 3 to 4 minutes or until spinach is hot and fish flakes
easily when tested with a fork.
Serve immediately.
Yield: 4 servings.

Per Serving: Calories 147 (19% from fat)   Fat 3.1g (sat 1.4g)   Protein 25.3g
Carbohydrate 4.4g   Fiber 2.3g   Cholesterol 48mg   Sodium 191mg
Exchanges: 3 Very Lean Meat

· · · · ·

HONEYBEE SUNDAES

total time: 4 minutes

Place ½ cup vanilla low-fat frozen yogurt in each of 4 dessert dishes.
Drizzle each serving with 1 tablespoon honey and 1 teaspoon sliced
almonds.
Yield: 4 servings.

Per Serving: Calories 159 (17% from fat)   Fat 3.0g (sat 1.3g)   Protein 3.0g
Carbohydrate 32.3g   Fiber 0.3g   Cholesterol 8mg   Sodium 29mg
Exchanges: 2 Starch, ½ Fat

Go Greek with feta-topped fish,

orzo (rice-shaped pasta), and Honeybee Sundaes.

Let the salad chill while you cook the fish.

For something sweet, offer fresh pineapple for dessert.

CITRUS-JERK ORANGE ROUGHY

total time: 9 minutes

4   (4-ounce) orange roughy fillets
1   tablespoon plus 1 teaspoon jerk seasoning
Cooking spray
1   teaspoon olive oil
4   tablespoons orange marmalade
3   tablespoons water
2   tablespoons lemon juice
⅛   teaspoon cracked pepper

Sprinkle both sides of fillets evenly with seasoning, pressing gently to adhere. Coat a large nonstick skillet with cooking spray; add oil, and place over medium-high heat until hot. Add fillets; cook 3 minutes on each side or until fish flakes easily when tested with a fork. Remove from skillet; set aside, and keep warm.
Add orange marmalade and remaining ingredients to skillet. Bring to a boil, and cook 1 minute. Pour sauce over fish, and serve immediately.
Yield: 4 servings.

Per Serving: Calories 151 (12% from fat)   Fat 2.0g (sat 0.2g)   Protein 17.1g
Carbohydrate 16.1g   Fiber 0.4g   Cholesterol 23mg   Sodium 142mg
Exchanges: 1 Starch, 2 Very Lean Meat

• • • • •

BLACK BEAN-RICE SALAD

total time: 10 minutes

Use 1 bag boil-in-bag rice to prepare 2 cups cooked rice.
Combine rice, 1 (15-ounce) can no-salt-added black beans, drained, and ¾ cup salsa. Cover and chill.
Yield: 4 (¾-cup servings).

Per Serving: Calories 259 (3% from fat)   Fat 0.8g (sat 0.2g)   Protein 11.9g
Carbohydrate 51.6g   Fiber 5.9g   Cholesterol 0mg   Sodium 141mg
Exchanges: 3 Starch, 1 Vegetable

Grocery List

4 cups fresh cubed pineapple

1 (15-ounce) can no-salt-added black beans

1 (8-ounce) jar salsa

Orange marmalade

Jerk seasoning

Cracked pepper

Olive oil

1 box boil-in-bag rice

Lemon juice

4 (4-ounce) orange roughy fillets

SUNFLOWER ORANGE ROUGHY

total time: 15 minutes

¼ cup corn flake crumbs
2 tablespoons dry roasted sunflower kernels
1 teaspoon salt-free seasoning
4 (4-ounce) orange roughy fillets
1 tablespoon lemon juice
Cooking spray

Combine first 3 ingredients in a small bowl. Dip fish in lemon juice, and dredge in crumb mixture.
Place fish on rack of a broiler pan coated with cooking spray. Sprinkle any remaining crumb mixture over fish. Bake at 425° for 10 minutes or until fish flakes easily when tested with a fork. Serve immediately.
Yield: 4 servings.

Per Serving: Calories 201 (40% from fat) Fat 9.0g (sat 1.3g) Protein 23.1g
Carbohydrate 6.0g Fiber 0.4g Cholesterol 68mg Sodium 112mg
Exchanges: ½ Starch, 3 Very Lean Meat, 1 Fat

• • • • •

GARLIC-DILL ROLLS

work time: 3 minutes • cook time: 15 minutes

Place rolls from 1 (11.3-ounce) can refrigerated roll dough on a baking sheet according to package directions. Combine 1½ tablespoons reduced-fat mayonnaise, 2 teaspoons dried dillweed, and ¼ teaspoon garlic powder in a small bowl. Brush mayonnaise mixture evenly over rolls, and bake at 375° for 15 minutes or until golden. (Store extra rolls in an airtight container, and serve with another meal.)
Yield: 8 rolls.

Per Roll: Calories 118 (21% from fat) Fat 2.8g (sat 0.1g) Protein 4.6g
Carbohydrate 18.3g Fiber 0.5g Cholesterol 1mg Sodium 291mg
Exchanges: 1 Starch, ½ Fat

Bake Garlic-Dill Rolls first and then steam some mixed vegetables while the fish bakes.

Grocery List

Dried dillweed

Garlic powder

Salt-free seasoning

1 (21-ounce) box corn flake crumbs

1 (3.75-ounce) package dry roasted sunflower kernels

Lemon juice

Reduced-fat mayonnaise

1 (11.3-ounce) can refrigerated roll dough

1 (16-ounce) package frozen mixed vegetables

4 (4-ounce) orange roughy fillets

Red Snapper Vera Cruz

total time: 12 minutes

Garlic-flavored or regular cooking spray
4 (4-ounce) red snapper or orange roughy fillets
½ teaspoon ground cumin
1 (8-ounce) can Mexican-style or regular stewed tomatoes,
     undrained
⅓ cup salsa
¼ cup chopped fresh cilantro or parsley

Coat a large nonstick skillet with cooking spray; place over medium-high heat until hot. Sprinkle one side of fillets with cumin.
Place fish, seasoned side down, in skillet; cook 3 minutes. Turn fish; top with tomatoes and salsa. Reduce heat, and simmer, uncovered, 5 minutes or until fish flakes easily when tested with a fork. Sprinkle with cilantro. Serve immediately.
Yield: 4 servings.

Per Serving: Calories 138 (12% from fat)   Fat 1.9g (sat 0.3g)   Protein 24.2g
Carbohydrate 5.0g   Fiber 0.8g   Cholesterol 42mg   Sodium 272mg
Exchanges: 1 Vegetable, 3 Very Lean Meat

• • • • •

Saffron Rice

total time: 15 minutes

Prepare 2 cups saffron rice according to package directions, using ⅔ cup rice and 1½ cups water, and omitting fat.
Yield: 4 (½-cup) servings.

Per Serving: Calories 95 (0% from fat)   Fat 0.0g (sat 0.0g)   Protein 2.0g
Carbohydrate 21.5g   Fiber 0.3g   Cholesterol 0mg   Sodium 485mg
Exchanges: 1½ Starch

Serve fish with rice and French rolls

so you can soak up the spicy sauce.

Grocery List

Fresh cilantro
or parsley

4 French rolls

1 (8-ounce) can
Mexican-style or regular
stewed tomatoes

1 (8-ounce) jar salsa

Cumin

1 (10-ounce) package
saffron rice mix

4 (4-ounce) red snapper
or orange roughy fillets

ORANGE-GLAZED SALMON

total time: 10 minutes

Grocery List

2 oranges

Low-sodium
soy sauce

Dark sesame oil

1 box boil-in-bag rice

Orange juice

2 (6-ounce) packages
frozen snow peas

4 (4-ounce) salmon fillets

4   (4-ounce) salmon fillets (1 inch thick)
¼   teaspoon salt
¼   teaspoon pepper
Cooking spray
3   tablespoons low-sodium soy sauce
3   tablespoons orange juice
½   teaspoon dark sesame oil

Sprinkle fish with salt and pepper. Coat a large nonstick skillet with cooking spray; place over high heat until hot. Add fish, and cook, uncovered, 3 minutes on each side. Cover and cook 3 additional minutes or until fish flakes easily when tested with a fork. Remove from skillet; set aside, and keep warm.
Add soy sauce and orange juice to skillet; cook over high heat 1 minute, stirring to deglaze skillet. Add oil, and stir well. Pour sauce over fish, and serve immediately.
Yield: 4 servings.

Per Serving: Calories 148 (28% from fat)   Fat 4.6g (sat 0.7g)   Protein 22.7g
Carbohydrate 1.3g   Fiber 0.1g   Cholesterol 59mg   Sodium 515mg
Exchanges: 3 Lean Meat

•   •   •   •   •

STEAMED SNOW PEAS

total time: 3 minutes

Place 2 (6-ounce) packages frozen snow peas in a microwave-safe bowl. Microwave at HIGH 3 to 4 minutes or until crisp-tender.
Yield: 4 servings.

Per Serving: Calories 36 (5% from fat)   Fat 0.2g (sat 0.0g)   Protein 2.3g
Carbohydrate 6.4g   Fiber 2.2g   Cholesterol 0mg   Sodium 3mg
Exchange: 1 Vegetable

Succulent salmon prepared in one skillet.

Steam snow peas and rice to go with the fish.

Game Plan: 1. Start the orzo on the stovetop.

2. Put the Lemon-Asparagus Packets on the grill.

3. After 5 minutes, put the salmon on the grill.

GRILLED HONEY-BALSAMIC SALMON

total time: 8 minutes

1½ tablespoons honey
1½ tablespoons Dijon mustard
1 tablespoon balsamic vinegar
¼ teaspoon coarsely ground pepper
¼ teaspoon garlic salt
2 (6-ounce) salmon steaks (½ inch thick)
Cooking spray

Combine first 5 ingredients in a bowl; brush mixture over fish.
Coat grill rack with cooking spray; place on grill over medium-hot coals (350° to 400°). Place fish on rack; grill, covered, 2 to 3 minutes on each side or until fish flakes easily when tested with a fork.
Serve immediately.
Yield: 2 servings.

Per Serving: Calories 256 (38% from fat)   Fat 10.7g (sat 1.7g)   Protein 24.2g
Carbohydrate 14.1g   Fiber 0.1g   Cholesterol 77mg   Sodium 655mg
Exchanges: 1 Starch, 3 Lean Meat

• • • • •

LEMON-ASPARAGUS PACKETS

total time: 12 minutes

Snap off tough ends of ½ pound asparagus; place asparagus on a square of heavy-duty aluminum foil. Spoon 2 teaspoons reduced-calorie margarine over asparagus, and sprinkle with ¼ teaspoon lemon-pepper seasoning. Fold aluminum foil tightly to seal. Place on grill rack, and grill over medium-hot coals 10 minutes.
Yield: 2 servings.

Per Serving: Calories 35 (67% from fat)   Fat 2.6g (sat 0.0g)   Protein 1.4g
Carbohydrate 2.9g   Fiber 1.3g   Cholesterol 0mg   Sodium 38mg
Exchanges: 1 Vegetable, ½ Fat

Grocery List

½ pound asparagus

Honey

Dijon mustard

Balsamic vinegar

Lemon-pepper seasoning

Garlic salt

1 (8-ounce) package orzo

Reduced-calorie margarine

2 (6-ounce) salmon steaks

2 lemons

2 medium zucchini

1 loaf French bread

1 (4½-ounce) jar minced garlic

Nonfat mayonnaise

Sweet pickle relish

Blackening seasoning

1 (8-ounce) can grated Parmesan cheese

4 (4-ounce) swordfish fillets

The flavor of blackened fish

without the smoke. Enjoy the spicy fish with Skillet Zucchini and French bread.

CAJUN-STYLE SWORDFISH

total time: 15 minutes

4   (4-ounce) swordfish fillets (1 inch thick)
Olive oil-flavored cooking spray
1½ teaspoons blackening seasoning, divided
⅓   cup nonfat mayonnaise
1   tablespoon sweet pickle relish
1   teaspoon fresh lemon juice
Lemon wedges (optional)

Coat both sides of fish with cooking spray; sprinkle evenly with
1¼ teaspoons blackening seasoning. Place fish on rack of a broiler
pan coated with cooking spray. Broil 5½ inches from heat 6 minutes
on each side or until fish flakes easily when tested with a fork.
While fish broils, combine mayonnaise, remaining ¼ teaspoon seasoning, relish, and lemon juice, stirring well. Serve fish immediately with
mayonnaise mixture and, if desired, lemon wedges.
Yield: 4 servings.

Per Serving: Calories 159 (27% from fat)   Fat 4.7g (sat 1.3g)   Protein 22.5g
Carbohydrate 5.4g   Fiber 0.0g   Cholesterol 44mg   Sodium 527mg
Exchanges: 3 Very Lean Meat

• • • • •

SKILLET ZUCCHINI

total time: 6 minutes

Coat a large nonstick skillet with olive oil-flavored cooking spray, and
place over medium heat. Add 1 teaspoon minced garlic, and sauté
1 minute. Add 2 medium zucchini, sliced and halved; sprinkle with
½ teaspoon salt and ¼ teaspoon pepper. Cook until zucchini is tender,
stirring occasionally. Sprinkle with 1 tablespoon Parmesan cheese.
Yield: 4 (½-cup) servings.

Per Serving: Calories 16 (28% from fat)   Fat 0.5g (sat 0.3g)   Protein 1.3g
Carbohydrate 2.3g   Fiber 0.3g   Cholesterol 1mg   Sodium 318mg
Exchange: 1 Vegetable

Celebrate spring with a primavera pasta,
whole wheat rolls, and strawberries.

TUNA PASTA PRIMAVERA

total time: 12 minutes

8   ounces bow tie pasta, uncooked
1   pound fresh asparagus
1   cup frozen English peas
¼   cup sliced green onions
½   teaspoon salt
2   teaspoons olive oil
1   cup seeded, chopped tomato
¼   cup lemon juice
2   (6-ounce) cans low-sodium white tuna packed in water,
       drained and coarsely flaked
½   teaspoon freshly ground pepper

Cook pasta according to package directions, omitting salt and fat; drain, reserving 3 tablespoons of pasta water.
While pasta cooks, snap off tough ends of asparagus. Remove scales from stalks, if desired. Cut asparagus into 1-inch pieces.
Combine asparagus and peas in a steamer basket over boiling water. Cover and steam 3 to 4 minutes or until asparagus is crisp-tender. Drain.
Combine steamed vegetables, green onions, salt, and olive oil in a large bowl. Add pasta, reserved pasta water, tomato, and lemon juice; toss well. Add tuna; toss. Sprinkle with freshly ground pepper.
Yield: 6 servings.

Per Serving: Calories 153 (14% from fat)   Fat 2.4g (sat 0.4g)   Protein 14.6g
Carbohydrate 18.8g   Fiber 2.7g   Cholesterol 12mg   Sodium 251mg
Exchanges: 1 Starch, 1 Vegetable, 1 Lean Meat

• • • • •

STRAWBERRIES AND CREAM

total time: 7 minutes

Sprinkle 2 teaspoons sugar over 4 cups sliced fresh strawberries. Combine 1½ cups thawed reduced-calorie frozen whipped topping and ½ teaspoon almond extract. Spoon strawberries evenly into 6 dessert dishes. Top evenly with whipped topping.
Yield: 6 servings.

Per Serving: Calories 72 (31% from fat)   Fat 2.5g (sat 0.0g)   Protein 1.1g
Carbohydrate 12.2g   Fiber 2.6g   Cholesterol 0mg   Sodium 13mg
Exchanges: 1 Fruit, ½ Fat

Grocery List

1 pound fresh asparagus

1 green onion

1 medium-size tomato

2 pints fresh strawberries

6 whole wheat French rolls

2 (6-ounce) cans low-sodium white tuna packed in water

Sugar

Almond extract

Olive oil

1 (8-ounce) package bow tie pasta

Lemon juice

1 (10-ounce) package frozen English peas

1 (12-ounce) container reduced-calorie frozen whipped topping

Grocery List

2 medium zucchini

4 rolls

1 (16-ounce) jar chunky
salsa

Salt-free garlic-herb
seasoning
(such as Mrs. Dash)

Olive oil

4 (4-ounce) tuna steaks

TUNA STEAKS WITH SALSA

total time: 7 minutes

4   (4-ounce) tuna steaks (½ inch thick)
Olive oil-flavored cooking spray
½   teaspoon salt-free garlic-herb seasoning
1   cup chunky salsa

Lightly coat both sides of fish with cooking spray; sprinkle both sides with seasoning. Coat a large nonstick skillet with cooking spray. Place over medium-high heat until hot. Add fish; cook 2 minutes on each side or to desired degree of doneness. Serve immediately with salsa.
Yield: 4 servings.

Per Serving: Calories 188 (29% from fat)   Fat 6.0g (sat 1.4g)   Protein 26.5g
Carbohydrate 6.2g   Fiber 0.1g   Cholesterol 43mg   Sodium 485mg
Exchanges: 1 Vegetable, 3½ Lean Meat

· · · · ·

ZUCCHINI STICKS

total time: 5 minutes

Coat a nonstick skillet with cooking spray; add 1 teaspoon olive oil, and place over medium-high heat until hot. Add 2 medium zucchini, sliced lengthwise into strips, and sauté 4 minutes or until crisp-tender.
Yield: 4 (½-cup) servings.

Per Serving: Calories 19 (66% from fat)   Fat 1.4g (sat 0.2g)   Protein 0.6g
Carbohydrate 1.6g   Fiber 0.3g   Cholesterol 0mg   Sodium 2mg
Exchange: 1 Vegetable

Fish doesn't get any easier.

Serve with Zucchini Sticks and rolls.

ANGEL HAIR PASTA WITH CLAMS

total time: 13 minutes

8 ounces angel hair pasta, uncooked
1 teaspoon olive oil
1½ teaspoons minced garlic
3 (6½-ounce) cans minced clams
2 tablespoons shredded fresh Parmesan cheese
Freshly ground pepper

Cook pasta according to package directions, omitting salt and fat.
While pasta cooks, heat oil in a large nonstick skillet over medium heat. Add garlic; sauté 2 minutes. Drain clams, reserving liquid. Add clam liquid to skillet, and simmer 5 minutes. Add clams; simmer 5 additional minutes.
Combine drained pasta and clam mixture in a serving bowl; toss gently. Sprinkle with cheese and pepper. Serve immediately.
Yield: 4 servings.

Per Serving: Calories 310 (11% from fat)   Fat 3.8g (sat 1.1g)   Protein 19.6g   Carbohydrate 47.0g   Fiber 1.4g   Cholesterol 47mg   Sodium 849mg
Exchanges: 3 Starch, 1 Lean Meat

Grocery List

1 loaf
French bread

3 (6½-ounce) cans
minced clams

1 (4½-ounce) jar
minced garlic

1 (8-ounce) package
angel hair pasta

Olive oil

1 (8-ounce) package
shredded fresh
Parmesan cheese

2 (10-ounce) packages
frozen broccoli spears

You may be surprised at what you can create with canned clams. Go for simple sides: steamed broccoli and French bread.

A saucy mussel dish in only 15 minutes
is hard to beat. Add a tossed green salad and Garlic Bread.

Linguine and Mussels Marinara

total time: 15 minutes

8   ounces linguine, uncooked
1   pound fresh, farm-raised mussels
2   cups low-fat chunky pasta sauce
¼   teaspoon crushed red pepper flakes
¼   cup chopped fresh basil

Cook pasta according to package directions, omitting salt and fat.
While pasta cooks, rinse mussels in cold water; remove beards on mussels, and scrub shells with a brush. Discard opened or cracked mussels. Combine mussels, pasta sauce, and red pepper flakes in a large deep skillet. Cover and bring to a simmer over medium heat; cook 5 minutes or until mussels open. (Discard any unopened mussels.)
Place ¾ cup drained pasta into each of 4 bowls. Top evenly with mussels and sauce; sprinkle with basil. Serve immediately.
Yield: 4 servings.

Per Serving: Calories 187 (10% from fat)   Fat 2.0g (sat 0.4g)   Protein 13.2g
Carbohydrate 27.9g   Fiber 3.0g   Cholesterol 20mg   Sodium 522mg
Exchanges: 2 Starch, 1 Lean Meat

• • • • •

Garlic Bread

total time: 12 minutes

Slice 1 (6-ounce) loaf French bread into 4 slices, and coat each slice with olive oil-flavored cooking spray. Spread 1 tablespoon minced garlic evenly over bread. Wrap loaf in aluminum foil, and bake at 350° for 10 minutes or until thoroughly heated.
Yield: 4 slices.

Per Slice: Calories 129 (8% from fat)   Fat 1.1g (sat 0.3g)   Protein 4.0g
Carbohydrate 24.3g   Fiber 1.0g   Cholesterol 1mg   Sodium 247mg
Exchanges: 1½ Starch

Grocery List

1 (10-ounce) package
mixed salad greens

Fresh basil

1 (6-ounce) loaf French
bread

1 (26-ounce) jar low-fat
chunky pasta sauce

1 (4½-ounce) jar
minced garlic

1 bottle low-fat
vinaigrette

Crushed
red pepper flakes

1 (8-ounce) package
linguine

1 pound fresh
farm-raised mussels

GRILLED SCALLOPS AND TOMATOES

total time: 18 minutes

1   pound fresh sea scallops
20 cherry tomatoes
Cooking spray
2   tablespoons low-sodium teriyaki sauce

Place scallops and tomatoes alternately on 4 (12-inch) skewers; brush with 1 tablespoon teriyaki sauce.
Coat grill rack with cooking spray; place on grill over medium-hot coals (350° to 400°). Place kabobs on rack, and grill, uncovered, 5 minutes. Turn kabobs, and brush with remaining teriyaki sauce; grill 10 additional minutes or until scallops are opaque. Serve immediately.
Yield: 4 servings.

Per Serving: Calories 123 (9% from fat)   Fat 1.2g (sat 0.1g)   Protein 20.0g
Carbohydrate 7.4g   Fiber 0.9g   Cholesterol 37mg   Sodium 349mg
Exchanges: 1 Vegetable, 3 Very Lean Meat

• • • • •

DILLED CORN ON THE COB

total time: 20 minutes

Coat 4 (6-inch) ears frozen corn with butter-flavored spray; sprinkle with minced fresh dillweed or dried dillweed. Place corn on grill rack, and grill, uncovered, 20 minutes or until corn is tender, turning occasionally.
Yield: 4 servings.

Per Serving: Calories 73 (15% from fat)   Fat 1.2g (sat 0.2g)   Protein 2.7g
Carbohydrate 15.7g   Fiber 2.6g   Cholesterol 0mg   Sodium 13mg
Exchange: 1 Starch

• • • • •

SPINACH-ONION SALAD

total time: 5 minutes

Combine 1 (10-ounce) package fresh spinach leaves, torn, with ½ purple onion, thinly sliced. Add ¼ cup fat-free red wine vinaigrette; toss.
Yield: 4 (1½-cup) servings.

Per Serving: Calories 41 (7% from fat)   Fat 0.3g (sat 0.1g)   Protein 2.2g
Carbohydrate 8.2g   Fiber 3.1g   Cholesterol 0mg   Sodium 277mg
Exchange: 1 Vegetable

An easy patio menu that's great for company!
Put the corn on the grill 5 minutes before the kabobs.

CHUNKY SHRIMP GAZPACHO

work time: 7 minutes • chill time: 10 minutes

3 cups water
1 pound peeled and deveined medium-size fresh shrimp
½ medium-size purple onion
1 small yellow squash
1 medium-size green pepper
3 (14-ounce) cans no-salt-added diced tomatoes
1 teaspoon herbes de Provence or ½ teaspoon dried thyme and
      ½ teaspoon dried tarragon
3 tablespoons picante sauce

Bring 3 cups water to a boil in a medium saucepan. Add shrimp; cook 3 to 5 minutes or until shrimp turn pink. Drain and rinse under cold water.

While shrimp cook, chop onion, squash, and pepper; place in a large bowl. Add cooked shrimp, tomatoes, herbs, and picante sauce to vegetable mixture, stirring well. Cover and chill at least 10 minutes.

Yield: 4 (1¾-cup) servings.

Per Serving: Calories 229 (9% from fat) Fat 2.2g (sat 0.4g) Protein 27.2g
Carbohydrate 26.3g Fiber 2.5g Cholesterol 172mg Sodium 347mg
Exchanges: 1 Starch, 2 Vegetable, 3 Very Lean Meat

Grocery List

1 medium-size
purple onion

1 small yellow squash

1 medium-size
green pepper

1 package focaccia

3 (14-ounce) cans
no-salt-added
diced tomatoes

1 (8-ounce) jar
picante sauce

Herbes de Provence or
dried thyme and dried
tarragon

1 pound peeled and
deveined medium-size
fresh shrimp

A chilled soup for a sweltering summer day.

Serve with focaccia wedges.

SWEET-AND-SOUR SHRIMP

total time: 9 minutes

1   (8-ounce) can pineapple chunks in juice
1   teaspoon cornstarch
3   tablespoons chili sauce
1   tablespoon low-sodium soy sauce
½   teaspoon garlic powder
Cooking spray
2   teaspoons sesame or vegetable oil
1   medium-size green pepper, coarsely chopped
½   medium onion, sliced
¾   pound peeled and deveined medium-size fresh shrimp

Drain pineapple, reserving juice; set pineapple chunks aside. Combine reserved juice, cornstarch, and next 3 ingredients; set aside.
Coat a large nonstick skillet or wok with cooking spray, and add oil. Place over medium-high heat until hot. Add green pepper and onion; stir-fry 2 to 3 minutes or until crisp-tender. Add shrimp; stir-fry 2 to 3 minutes or until shrimp turn pink.
Stir cornstarch mixture and pineapple chunks into shrimp mixture. Cook over medium heat, stirring constantly, until mixture is thickened and bubbly. Serve immediately.
Yield: 4 servings.

Per Serving: Calories 177 (20% from fat)   Fat 4.0g (sat 0.7g)   Protein 18.0g
Carbohydrate 16.2g   Fiber 0.8g   Cholesterol 129mg   Sodium 397mg
Exchanges: 1 Starch, 2 Lean Meat

• • • • •

BAKED WONTON CRISPS

total time: 10 minutes

Combine 1½ teaspoons sesame or vegetable oil with 1½ teaspoons water; brush evenly over 12 wonton skins on a baking sheet. Sprinkle 1½ teaspoons sesame seeds and ¼ teaspoon salt evenly over wonton skins. Bake at 400° for 5 minutes or until lightly browned and crisp.
Yield: 4 servings (serving size: 3 crisps).

Per Serving: Calories 79 (30% from fat)   Fat 2.6g (sat 0.4g)   Protein 2.1g
Carbohydrate 11.7g   Fiber 0.1g   Cholesterol 2mg   Sodium 260mg
Exchanges: 1 Starch, ½ Fat

An extra-saucy stir-fry, so cook some rice
to spoon it over. Baked Wonton Crisps are a tasty, low-fat
alternative to fried Chinese noodles.

POLENTA WITH SHRIMP AND TOMATO SAUCE

total time: 15 minutes

Olive oil-flavored cooking spray
1   (16-ounce) package refrigerated polenta, cut into 12 slices
¾ pound peeled and deveined medium-size fresh shrimp
2   cups low-fat chunky pasta sauce
3   tablespoons shredded fresh Parmesan cheese

Coat a large nonstick skillet with cooking spray; place over medium-high heat until hot.

Arrange polenta slices in skillet; cook 4 minutes on each side or until edges are crisp. Remove from skillet, and keep warm.

Coat skillet with cooking spray. Add shrimp, and cook 2 to 3 minutes or until shrimp turn pink. Stir in pasta sauce; cook 2 to 3 minutes or until thoroughly heated.

Place 3 slices of polenta on each of 4 serving plates. Spoon shrimp and sauce evenly over polenta; sprinkle with Parmesan cheese. Serve immediately.

Yield: 4 servings.

Per Serving: Calories 238 (11% from fat)   Fat 3.0g (sat 1.2g)   Protein 23.2g
Carbohydrate 26.0g   Fiber 4.0g   Cholesterol 133mg   Sodium 799mg
Exchanges: 2 Starch, 2½ Very Lean Meat

Grocery List

1 (10-ounce) package mixed salad greens

1 (26-ounce) jar low-fat chunky pasta sauce

1 bottle low-fat olive-oil vinaigrette

1 (8-ounce) package shredded fresh Parmesan cheese

1 (16-ounce) package refrigerated polenta

¾ pound peeled and deveined medium-size fresh shrimp

Great time savers—refrigerated polenta

and greens in a bag for a salad.

Grocery List

1 (10-ounce) package mixed salad greens

1 loaf sourdough bread

1 (14½-ounce) can diced tomatoes with roasted garlic

1 bottle low-fat vinaigrette

Blackening seasoning

1 (8-ounce) package fettuccine

Olive oil

Lemon juice

¾ pound peeled and deveined large fresh shrimp

ZESTY FETTUCCINE AND SHRIMP

total time: 9 minutes

8   ounces fettuccine, uncooked
Olive oil-flavored cooking spray
2   teaspoons olive oil
2   teaspoons blackening seasoning
¾   pound peeled and deveined large fresh shrimp
2   tablespoons lemon juice
1   (14½-ounce) can diced tomatoes with roasted garlic, drained
¼   teaspoon pepper

Cook pasta according to package directions, omitting salt and fat.
While pasta cooks, coat a large nonstick skillet with cooking spray, and add oil. Place over medium-high heat until hot. Sprinkle blackening seasoning evenly over shrimp. Add shrimp to skillet; cook 2 minutes on each side or until shrimp turn pink. Stir in lemon juice. Add tomatoes and pepper; cook until thoroughly heated.
Spoon shrimp mixture over drained pasta, and serve immediately.
Yield: 4 servings.

Per Serving: Calories 344 (13% from fat)   Fat 4.9g (sat 0.7g)   Protein 25.2g
Carbohydrate 48.2g   Fiber 1.7g   Cholesterol 129mg   Sodium 492mg
Exchanges: 3 Starch, 2 Lean Meat

Unbelievable flavor in less than 10 minutes.

The shrimp is good with a tossed green salad and sourdough bread.

Skillet Ziti and Vegetables, page 66

Nearly half of all shoppers buy precut, cleaned, and ready-to-cook vegetables and precut, packaged salads.

Meatless Main Dishes

Key ingredients for meatless meals:

- variety of pastas

- pasta sauces

- frozen vegetables

- canned beans

- preshredded cheeses

CONFETTI CHEESE OMELET

total time: 14 minutes

Cooking spray
¼ cup chopped sweet red pepper
¼ cup chopped green or sweet orange pepper
¼ cup sliced green onions
1 cup fat-free egg substitute
¼ teaspoon salt
¼ teaspoon freshly ground pepper
½ cup (2 ounces) shredded reduced-fat Cheddar cheese

Coat a 10-inch nonstick skillet with cooking spray; place over medium heat until hot. Add peppers and onions; cook 4 minutes, stirring occasionally.
Pour egg substitute into skillet; sprinkle with salt and pepper. Cook, without stirring, 2 to 3 minutes or until golden brown on bottom. Sprinkle with cheese. Loosen omelet with a spatula; fold in half. Cook 2 additional minutes or until egg mixture is set and cheese begins to melt.
Cut omelet in half. Slide halves onto serving plates.
Yield: 2 servings.

Per Serving: Calories 159 (33% from fat)   Fat 5.9g (sat 3.2g)   Protein 20.7g
Carbohydrate 5.3g   Fiber 0.7g   Cholesterol 19mg   Sodium 680mg
Exchanges: 1 Vegetable, 3 Lean Meat

Grocery List

1 medium-size sweet red pepper

1 medium-size green or sweet orange pepper

1 green onion

1 pint fresh strawberries

1 package English muffins

Spreadable fruit (such as Polaner's)

Coffee

1 (8-ounce) carton fat-free egg substitute

1 (8-ounce) package shredded reduced-fat Cheddar cheese

Saturday morning special: a cheesy omelet, toasted English muffins, and fresh strawberries.

Don't forget the coffee.

CHEESY BEAN CASSEROLE

total time: 16 minutes

Grocery List

1 small onion

2 (15-ounce) cans
chile-hot kidney beans

2 (14½-ounce) cans
no-salt-added whole
tomatoes

Garlic powder

1 (7.5-ounce) package
yellow corn muffin mix

1 (8-ounce) package
shredded reduced-fat
sharp Cheddar cheese

Cooking spray
1   cup chopped onion
2   (15-ounce) cans chile-hot kidney beans, drained
2   (14½-ounce) cans no-salt-added whole tomatoes, drained and
        chopped
½   teaspoon garlic powder
¼   teaspoon pepper
1   cup (4 ounces) shredded reduced-fat sharp Cheddar cheese

Coat a nonstick skillet with cooking spray; place over medium-high
heat until hot. Add onion; sauté until tender. Stir in beans and next
3 ingredients. Cook 3 minutes or until thoroughly heated, stirring well.
Spoon mixture into 4 individual baking dishes or 1 (8-inch) square
baking dish; sprinkle with cheese. Bake, uncovered, at 400° for 5 minutes or until cheese melts. Let stand 5 minutes.
Yield: 4 servings.

Per Serving: Calories 231 (25% from fat)   Fat 6.5g (sat 3.6g)   Protein 15.1g
Carbohydrate 27.7g   Fiber 6.8g   Cholesterol 19mg   Sodium 643mg
Exchanges: 2 Starch, 1 Medium-Fat Meat

• • • • •

SKILLET CORNBREAD

total time: 18 minutes

Prepare 1 (7.5-ounce) package yellow corn muffin mix according to
package directions using ½ cup water. Pour batter into an 8-inch
ovenproof skillet coated with cooking spray, and bake at 400° for
16 minutes or until golden. Cut into wedges.
Yield: 6 wedges.

Per Wedge: Calories 133 (20% from fat)   Fat 2.9g (sat 0.8g)   Protein 1.7g
Carbohydrate 25.8g   Fiber 0.4g   Cholesterol 0mg   Sodium 233mg
Exchanges: 1½ Starch, ½ Fat

While the cornbread bakes, make the casserole.
Put it in the oven with the cornbread the last 5 minutes of baking.

SOUTHWESTERN VEGETABLE BAKE

work time: 5 minutes • cook time: 25 minutes

2   (10-ounce) packages frozen Southwestern-style corn and roasted red peppers, thawed
1   (14½-ounce) can chili-style tomatoes, undrained
1   (15½-ounce) can white hominy, drained
1   (15-ounce) can no-salt-added black beans, rinsed and drained
¼   teaspoon pepper
½   cup (2 ounces) shredded Pepper-Jack cheese

Combine first 5 ingredients in a 2-quart baking dish; stir well. Cover and bake at 350° for 25 minutes or until bubbly. Uncover, sprinkle with cheese, and bake 5 additional minutes.
Yield: 4 servings.

Per Serving: Calories 364 (16% from fat)   Fat 6.5g (sat 2.8g)   Protein 16.6g   Carbohydrate 62.7g   Fiber 8.3g   Cholesterol 11mg   Sodium 958mg
Exchanges: 3 Starch, 3 Vegetable

• • • • •

TORTILLA WEDGES

total time: 8 minutes

Cut 4 (8-inch) flour tortillas into wedges, and coat with butter-flavored cooking spray. Bake at 400° for 4 to 5 minutes or until lightly browned and crisp.
Yield: 4 servings (serving size: 4 wedges).

Per Serving: Calories 140 (21% from fat)   Fat 3.2g (sat 0.5g)   Protein 3.7g   Carbohydrate 23.6g   Fiber 1.3g   Cholesterol 0mg   Sodium 203mg
Exchanges: 1½ Starch, ½ Fat

Grocery List

1 (14½-ounce) can chili-style tomatoes

1 (15½-ounce) can white hominy

1 (15-ounce) can no-salt-added black beans

1 (8-ounce) package shredded Pepper-Jack cheese

1 package 8-inch flour tortillas

2 (10-ounce) packages frozen Southwestern-style corn and roasted red peppers

Dump the vegetables into a baking dish,

and go read the next chapter in your book

while the casserole bakes.

VEGETARIAN TACOS

total time: 14 minutes

1½ cups frozen burger-style vegetable protein crumbles, thawed
1 (8-ounce) can no-salt-added tomato sauce
1 small onion, chopped
1 teaspoon minced garlic
2 teaspoons chili powder
1 teaspoon ground cumin
8 taco shells
Taco Bar Toppings

Combine first 6 ingredients in a medium saucepan. Bring to a boil; cover, reduce heat, and simmer 10 minutes or until mixture is thoroughly heated. While protein crumble mixture cooks, prepare Taco Bar Toppings.

Spoon mixture evenly into taco shells. Serve with toppings, as desired.

Yield: 4 servings (serving size: 2 tacos).

Note: Nutrient values will vary according to choice of toppings. Analysis reflects tacos in photograph.

Per Serving: Calories 334 (34% from fat) Fat 12.5g (sat 3.8g) Protein 20.3g
Carbohydrate 34.4g Fiber 6.1g Cholesterol 17mg Sodium 494mg
Exchanges: 2 Starch, 1 Vegetable, 2 Medium-Fat Meat

• • • • •

TACO BAR TOPPINGS

1 small onion, chopped
1 green pepper, chopped
½ head lettuce, shredded
½ (10-ounce) package shredded carrots
½ (6-ounce) package radishes, sliced
1 (15-ounce) can no-salt-added black beans, rinsed and drained
½ (16-ounce) jar salsa
½ (8-ounce) package shredded reduced-fat Cheddar cheese
½ (8-ounce) package shredded part-skim mozzarella cheese

Place toppings in individual serving dishes, and top tacos as desired.

Yield: 4 servings.

A Taco Bar is a great supper club idea.

For dessert, let everyone make their own

Neapolitan Sundae! (page 221).

Grocery List

2 medium-size
yellow squash

2 medium zucchini

1 package focaccia
or loaf French bread

1 (7-ounce) jar roasted
red peppers

1 (2.8-ounce) container
pesto

1 (8-ounce) package
shredded fresh
Parmesan cheese

1 (16-ounce) package
sun-dried tomato-
flavored polenta

SUMMER SQUASH SAUTÉ OVER POLENTA

total time: 15 minutes

Garlic-flavored cooking spray
1 (16-ounce) package sun-dried tomato-flavored polenta,
      cut into 12 slices
2 tablespoons pesto
2 tablespoons water
2 cups sliced yellow squash
2 cups sliced zucchini
1 (7-ounce) jar roasted red peppers, drained and cut into strips
½ cup (2 ounces) shredded fresh Parmesan cheese

Place polenta slices on a baking sheet coated with cooking spray. Broil
3½ inches from heat 5 minutes on each side or until lightly browned.
While polenta bakes, coat a large nonstick skillet with cooking spray;
place skillet over medium-high heat until hot. Add pesto and water, stirring well. Add yellow squash and zucchini; cover and cook 5 minutes
or until vegetables are tender. Add red peppers; cook until thoroughly
heated.
To serve, spoon zucchini mixture evenly over polenta, and sprinkle
with cheese.
Yield: 4 servings.

Per Serving: Calories 197 (27% from fat)   Fat 5.9g (sat 2.8g)   Protein 9.9g
Carbohydrate 26.6g   Fiber 3.8g   Cholesterol 10mg   Sodium 559mg
Exchanges: 1 Starch, 2 Vegetable, 1 Fat

Add warm focaccia wedges

or French bread for a simple veggie supper.

COUSCOUS SALAD

total time: 15 minutes

½ (16-ounce) package frozen broccoli stir-fry vegetables
1¼ cups water
1 (10-ounce) package garlic-flavored couscous
¼ cup fat-free Caesar salad dressing, divided
1 (10-ounce) package fresh spinach
½ cup (2 ounces) crumbled feta cheese

Combine vegetables, water, and seasoning packet from couscous in a large saucepan; bring to a boil. Add couscous, stirring well. Remove from heat; cover and let stand 5 minutes or until liquid is absorbed. Stir in 1 tablespoon dressing.

While couscous stands, remove and discard stems from spinach. Wash spinach, and pat dry with paper towels. Slice spinach, and place in a large bowl. Drizzle remaining 3 tablespoons dressing over spinach, and toss well.

Spoon couscous mixture over spinach, and sprinkle with cheese.

Yield: 4 servings.

Per Serving: Calories 241 (17% from fat)   Fat 4.5g (sat 2.2g)   Protein 10.9g
Carbohydrate 42.7g   Fiber 5.1g   Cholesterol 13mg   Sodium 731mg
Exchanges: 2 Starch, 2 Vegetable, 1 Fat

• • • • •

BAKED PITA WEDGES

total time: 10 minutes

Split 2 pita bread rounds in half horizontally. Cut each half into 8 wedges. Arrange wedges, cut sides up, on a baking sheet. Sprinkle with 1 teaspoon Greek seasoning, and generously coat with olive oil-flavored cooking spray. Bake at 400° for 6 to 7 minutes or until crisp.

Yield: 4 servings (serving size: 8 wedges).

Per Serving: Calories 77 (11% from fat)   Fat 0.9g (sat 0.0g)   Protein 1.4g
Carbohydrate 14.1g   Fiber 2.6g   Cholesterol 0mg   Sodium 349mg
Exchange: 1 Starch

Grocery List

1 (10-ounce) package
fresh spinach

1 pound red grapes

1 package pita bread
rounds

1 bottle fat-free Caesar
salad dressing

Greek seasoning

1 (10-ounce) package
garlic-flavored couscous

1 (4-ounce) package
crumbled feta cheese

1 (16-ounce) package
frozen broccoli stir-fry
vegetables

A hearty meat-free salad with crispy chips.

Enjoy red grapes after your meal.

MEDITERRANEAN PASTA WITH ZUCCHINI

total time: 13 minutes

8   ounces penne or ziti pasta, uncooked
1   (14½-ounce) can diced tomatoes with basil, garlic, and oregano
1   (15-ounce) can chickpeas, drained
1   medium zucchini, sliced
2   tablespoons sliced ripe olives

Cook pasta according to package directions, omitting salt and fat.
While pasta cooks, combine tomatoes and remaining 3 ingredients
in a large skillet; bring to a boil. Reduce heat, and simmer, uncovered,
5 minutes.
Spoon tomato mixture over drained pasta.
Yield: 4 (2-cup) servings.

Per Serving: Calories 363 (9% from fat)   Fat 3.6g (sat 0.3g)   Protein 14.4g
Carbohydrate 67.5g   Fiber 3.2g   Cholesterol 0mg   Sodium 458mg
Exchanges: 4 Starch, 1 Vegetable, ½ Fat

Grocery List

4 fresh pears

1 medium zucchini

1 package pita bread
rounds

1 (14½-ounce) can diced
tomatoes with basil,
garlic, and oregano

1 (15-ounce) can
chickpeas

1 (2¼-ounce) can sliced
ripe olives

1 (8-ounce) package
penne or ziti pasta

A one-dish Mediterranean-style meal.

Serve with pita bread and fresh pears.

SKILLET ZITI AND VEGETABLES

work time: 5 minutes • cook time: 15 minutes

Grocery List

1 (10-ounce) package
fresh stir-fry vegetables

6 rolls

1 (26-ounce) jar low-fat
sun-dried tomato and
herb pasta sauce
(such as Healthy Choice)

1 (8-ounce) package
ziti pasta

1 (8-ounce) package
shredded provolone
cheese

½ gallon fat-free
ice cream

2 cups low-fat sun-dried tomato and herb pasta sauce
2 cups water
8 ounces ziti pasta, uncooked
1 (10-ounce) package fresh stir-fry vegetables (about 2½ cups)
¾ cup (3 ounces) shredded provolone cheese

Combine pasta sauce and water in a large skillet; bring to a boil. Add pasta and vegetables. Cover, reduce heat, and simmer 15 minutes or until pasta is tender.
Remove from heat, and sprinkle with cheese.
Yield: 6 (1¼-cup) servings.

Per Serving: Calories 244 (18% from fat)   Fat 4.9g (sat 2.5g)   Protein 11.2g
Carbohydrate 39.6g   Fiber 4.1g   Cholesterol 10mg   Sodium 395mg
Exchanges: 2 Starch, 2 Vegetable, 1 Fat

You only have to use one skillet
for dinner. Serve crusty rolls with the pasta,
and for dessert—fat-free ice cream.

Fettuccine with Blue Cheese-Artichoke Sauce

total time: 15 minutes

1   (9-ounce) package refrigerated fettuccine
Cooking spray
1   (14-ounce) can quartered artichoke hearts, drained
1   cup sliced fresh mushrooms
1   (10-ounce) container refrigerated light alfredo sauce
2   tablespoons crumbled blue cheese

Cook pasta according to package directions, omitting salt and fat.
While pasta cooks, coat a large nonstick skillet with cooking spray;
place over medium-high heat until hot. Add artichokes and mushrooms;
cook 3 to 4 minutes or until mushrooms are tender. Add alfredo sauce
to artichoke mixture; cook until thoroughly heated.
Place drained pasta in a large bowl. Pour sauce mixture over pasta;
toss to combine. Sprinkle with cheese.
Yield: 4 (1¼-cup) servings.

Per Serving: Calories 313 (24% from fat)   Fat 8.5g (sat 4.1g)   Protein 14.7g
Carbohydrate 45.7g   Fiber 2.6g   Cholesterol 25mg   Sodium 691mg
Exchanges: 3 Starch, 1 High-Fat Meat

· · · · ·

Tossed Apple Salad

total time: 5 minutes

Combine ½ (10-ounce) package romaine lettuce and 1 cup diced Red
Delicious apple in a bowl. Drizzle with ⅓ cup fat-free balsamic vinaigrette.
Yield: 4 (1¼-cup) servings.

Per Serving: Calories 42 (4% from fat)   Fat 0.2g (sat 0.0g)   Protein 0.6g
Carbohydrate 9.9g   Fiber 1.6g   Cholesterol 0mg   Sodium 268mg
Exchange: ½ Fruit

Creamy. Cheesy. Yum!

Tossed Apple Salad, or just sliced apples,

and soft breadsticks complement the pasta.

Grocery List

1 (8-ounce) package
sliced fresh mushrooms

1 (10-ounce) package
romaine lettuce

1 Red Delicious apple

1 package soft
breadsticks

1 (14-ounce) can
quartered artichoke
hearts

1 bottle fat-free balsamic
vinaigrette

1 (10-ounce) container
refrigerated
light alfredo sauce

1 (9-ounce) package
refrigerated fettuccine

1 (4-ounce) package
crumbled blue cheese

TORTELLINI PRIMAVERA WITH PESTO SAUCE

total time: 13 minutes

Grocery List

1 package soft Italian
breadsticks

1 (2.8-ounce) container
pesto

1 (9-ounce) package
refrigerated cheese
tortellini

1 (8-ounce) package
shredded fresh
Parmesan cheese

1 (8-ounce) container
fat-free sour cream

1 (16-ounce) package
frozen broccoli stir-fry
vegetables

1   (9-ounce) package refrigerated cheese tortellini
1   (16-ounce) package frozen broccoli stir-fry vegetables
1   (8-ounce) container fat-free sour cream
2   tablespoons pesto
¼   teaspoon salt
¼   cup (1 ounce) shredded fresh Parmesan cheese
⅛   teaspoon freshly ground pepper

Cook tortellini and vegetables in 3 quarts boiling water 5 to 7 minutes
or until vegetables and pasta are tender. Drain and return to pan.
Combine sour cream, pesto, and salt, stirring well. Gently stir sour
cream mixture into pasta mixture. Sprinkle with Parmesan cheese and
pepper. Serve immediately.
Yield: 4 (1¼-cup) servings.

Per Serving: Calories 331 (33% from fat)   Fat 12.2g (sat 4.5g)   Protein 18.7g
Carbohydrate 38.1g   Fiber 3.0g   Cholesterol 32mg   Sodium 659mg
Exchanges: 2 Starch, 2 Vegetable, 1 High-Fat Meat, 1 Fat

For simple sides to go with your pasta,
try **Marinated Cucumbers and Tomatoes** (page 215)
and soft Italian breadsticks.

Grocery List

4 plum tomatoes

1 medium-size purple onion

Fresh basil or oregano

1 large head Bibb lettuce

1 (6-ounce) package radishes

1 (16-ounce) package cauliflower flowerets

1 (10-ounce) thin-crust Italian bread shell (such as Boboli)

1 (15.8-ounce) can Great Northern beans

1 bottle fat-free vinaigrette

1 (4-ounce) package crumbled Gorgonzola cheese or blue cheese

FRESH TOMATO PIZZA

total time: 15 minutes

1   (10-ounce) thin-crust Italian bread shell
Olive oil-flavored cooking spray
4   plum tomatoes, thinly sliced
½   medium-size purple onion, thinly sliced
½   cup (2 ounces) crumbled Gorgonzola cheese or blue cheese
¼   cup chopped fresh basil or oregano

Place bread shell on an ungreased baking sheet or pizza pan; coat crust with cooking spray. Top with tomato and remaining ingredients. Bake at 425° for 7 to 8 minutes or until cheese melts. Cut into wedges, and serve immediately.
Yield: 4 servings.

Per Serving: Calories 279 (31% from fat)   Fat 9.5g (sat 2.7g)   Protein 11.5g
Carbohydrate 36.4g   Fiber 2.1g   Cholesterol 11mg   Sodium 592mg
Exchanges: 2 Starch, 1 Vegetable, 1 High-Fat Meat

• • • • •

CRUNCHY RADISH-CAULIFLOWER SALAD

total time: 5 minutes

Combine 1 large head Bibb lettuce, chopped; 1 (6-ounce) package radishes, sliced; 1 cup small cauliflower flowerets; 1 (15.8-ounce) can Great Northern beans, drained and rinsed; and ⅓ cup fat-free vinaigrette in a large bowl; toss gently.
Yield: 4 (1½-cup) servings.

Per Serving: Calories 143 (5% from fat)   Fat 0.9g (sat 0.1g)   Protein 7.8g
Carbohydrate 26.2g   Fiber 7.5g   Cholesterol 0mg   Sodium 491mg
Exchanges: 1 Starch, 2 Vegetable

Pizza and salad . . . too good to be healthy. It's all you need for dinner.

Mushroom Pizza

total time: 15 minutes

Grocery List

1 (16-ounce) package
baby carrots

1 stalk celery

1 (16-ounce) package
broccoli flowerets

12 cherry tomatoes

1 (8-ounce) package
sliced fresh mushrooms

1 (14-ounce) jar
pizza sauce

1 bottle fat-free
Ranch-style dressing

Dried Italian seasoning

1 (10-ounce) refrigerated
pizza crust dough

1 (8-ounce) package
shredded part-skim
mozzarella cheese

1   (10-ounce) can refrigerated pizza crust dough
Cooking spray
1   teaspoon dried Italian seasoning
½   cup pizza sauce
1   (8-ounce) package sliced fresh mushrooms
1¼ cups (5 ounces) shredded part-skim mozzarella cheese

Unroll pizza crust dough, and place on a baking sheet coated with cooking spray; press to a 14- x 10-inch rectangle. Sprinkle dough with Italian seasoning. Bake at 425° for 7 minutes.

Spread pizza sauce over crust; top with mushrooms. Sprinkle with cheese. Bake 6 additional minutes or until cheese melts.

To serve, cut pizza into squares.

Yield: 4 servings.

Per Serving: Calories 315 (27% from fat)   Fat 9.4g (sat 3.6g)   Protein 16.6g
Carbohydrate 40.2g   Fiber 2.6g   Cholesterol 21mg   Sodium 833mg
Exchanges: 2 Starch, 2 Vegetable, 1 High-Fat Meat

Your kids will love
these hand-sized pizza squares.
Set out a fresh veggie tray with fat-free dressing, and
serve **Chocolate Chip Frozen Yogurt** (page 221)
for dessert.

Grocery List

1 head romaine lettuce

12 cherry tomatoes

1 purple onion

2 bagels

1 bottle fat-free
French dressing

1 (7.6-ounce) package
roasted garlic instant
mashed potatoes

1 (8-ounce) package
shredded reduced-fat
sharp Cheddar cheese

Fat-free milk

A creamy, high-flavor soup.

Much better than opening a can. Serve with

Romaine Salad and Bagel Chips. They're easy to

make and hard to resist.

ROASTED GARLIC-POTATO SOUP

total time: 13 minutes

2   cups fat-free milk
1½   cups water
½   (7.6-ounce) package roasted garlic instant mashed potatoes
1   cup (4 ounces) shredded reduced-fat sharp Cheddar cheese,
         divided
¼   teaspoon freshly ground pepper

Combine milk and water in a large saucepan; bring to a boil. Remove from heat; add potatoes, and stir with a wire whisk until well blended. **Add** ¾ cup cheese, stirring until cheese melts. Spoon evenly into 4 bowls; sprinkle evenly with remaining ¼ cup cheese and pepper.
Yield: 4 (1-cup) servings.

Per Serving: Calories 219 (31% from fat)   Fat 7.6g (sat 3.8g)   Protein 14.5g
Carbohydrate 25.2g   Fiber 1.0g   Cholesterol 22mg   Sodium 609mg
Exchanges: 1½ Starch, 1 High-Fat Meat

• • • • •

ROMAINE SALAD

total time: 5 minutes

Combine 4 cups shredded romaine lettuce, 12 cherry tomatoes, halved, and 1 purple onion, sliced. Drizzle with ½ cup fat-free French dressing; toss.
Yield: 4 (1¼-cup) servings.

Per Serving: Calories 81 (3% from fat)   Fat 0.3g (sat 0.0g)   Protein 1.7g
Carbohydrate 18.3g   Fiber 2.1g   Cholesterol 0mg   Sodium 309mg
Exchanges: 1 Starch, 1 Vegetable

• • • • •

BAGEL CHIPS

total time: 10 minutes

Slice 2 bagels into thin slices, using a serrated knife. Coat slices with butter-flavored cooking spray. Bake at 350° for 5 minutes or until crisp.
Yield: 4 servings.

Per Serving: Calories 140 (8% from fat)   Fat 1.2g (sat 0.1g)   Protein 5.2g
Carbohydrate 26.5g   Fiber 1.0g   Cholesterol 0mg   Sodium 265mg
Exchanges: 2 Starch

Grocery List

2 green onions

1 (14¼-ounce) can
fat-free, reduced-sodium
chicken broth or
vegetable broth

Chili powder

1 package reduced-fat
biscuit and baking mix
(such as Bisquick)

1 carton fat-free
half-and-half or 1 can
fat-free evaporated milk

1 (8-ounce) loaf
reduced-fat process
cheese spread
(such as light Velveeta)

Fat-free milk

1 (16-ounce) package
frozen broccoli, corn,
and red peppers

1 (24-ounce) package
frozen potatoes O'Brien
with onions and peppers

CREAMY VEGETABLE SOUP

total time: 15 minutes

1 (16-ounce) package frozen broccoli, corn, and red peppers
3 cups frozen potatoes O'Brien with onions and peppers
1 (14¼-ounce) can fat-free, reduced-sodium chicken broth or
    vegetable broth
1 cup fat-free half-and-half or fat-free evaporated milk
½ (8-ounce) loaf reduced-fat process cheese spread, cubed
¼ teaspoon pepper

Combine first 3 ingredients in a large saucepan; bring to a boil. Cover, reduce heat, and simmer 6 minutes or until vegetables are tender. Stir in half-and-half and cheese; continue stirring until cheese melts and soup is thoroughly heated. Stir in pepper, and serve immediately.
Yield: 4 (1½-cup) servings.

Per Serving: Calories 250 (13% from fat) Fat 3.6g (sat 2.1g) Protein 12.0g
Carbohydrate 39.2g Fiber 6.3g Cholesterol 10mg Sodium 643mg
Exchanges: 2 Starch, 2 Vegetable, 1 Fat

• • • • •

CHILI-ONION DROP BISCUITS

total time: 10 minutes

Combine 1 cup reduced-fat biscuit and baking mix, ⅓ cup fat-free milk, 2 green onions, chopped, and 1 teaspoon chili powder in a bowl; stir just until dry ingredients are moistened. Drop dough onto a baking sheet coated with cooking spray. Bake at 450° for 7 minutes or until golden.
Yield: 6 biscuits.

Per Biscuit: Calories 83 (15% from fat) Fat 1.4g (sat 0.3g) Protein 2.1g
Carbohydrate 15.3g Fiber 0.5g Cholesterol 0mg Sodium 242mg
Exchange: 1 Starch

Stir up the biscuit dough first,

then bake the biscuits while the

soup is simmering.

TOMATO-CHEESE RAVIOLI SOUP

total time: 13 minutes

1   (14½-ounce) can stewed tomatoes
1   (14¼-ounce) can fat-free, reduced-sodium chicken broth or
        vegetable broth
½   teaspoon dried Italian seasoning
3   cups frozen cheese ravioli or fresh cheese tortellini (about 12 ounces)
1   small zucchini, sliced
¼   teaspoon freshly ground pepper

Combine first 3 ingredients in a large saucepan; bring to a boil. Cover,
reduce heat, and simmer 5 minutes. Add ravioli, zucchini, and pepper;
bring to a boil. Cover, reduce heat, and simmer 7 to 8 minutes or until
pasta and zucchini are tender.
Yield: 4 (1¼-cup) servings.

Per Serving: Calories 317 (18% from fat)   Fat 6.3g (sat 2.0g)   Protein 14.6g
Carbohydrate 47.9g   Fiber 0.7g   Cholesterol 39mg   Sodium 653mg
Exchanges: 3 Starch, 1 Medium-Fat Meat

Grocery List

1 small zucchini

1 (14½-ounce) can
stewed tomatoes

1 (14¼-ounce) can
fat-free, reduced-sodium
chicken broth or
vegetable broth

Dried Italian seasoning

1 box low-fat crackers

3 (9-ounce) packages
frozen cheese ravioli or
fresh cheese tortellini

You don't need anything else to go
with this chunky soup except a stack of
low-fat crackers. But if you must have dessert,
the **Brownie Sundae** (page 223) is delicious.

Deep-Dish Pizza Casserole, page 90

9 out of 10 households serve beef in an average two-week period.

Meats

Keep these quick-fix meats in your freezer so you'll always have the makings for a hearty and healthy meal:

- ground round
- boneless top sirloin
- flank steak
- lamb chops
- boneless pork chops
- pork tenderloin

ROAST BEEF AND BLUE CHEESE SALAD

total time: 7 minutes

8 cups packed European-style mixed salad greens
8 ounces thinly sliced, well-trimmed deli roast beef
20 cherry tomatoes
¼ cup (1 ounce) crumbled blue cheese
⅓ cup fat-free raspberry vinaigrette

Arrange salad greens evenly on each of 4 plates.
Divide roast beef slices into 2 stacks; roll each stack, jellyroll fashion, and cut crosswise into 1-inch slices.
Arrange beef, tomatoes, and cheese over greens. Drizzle evenly with vinaigrette.
Yield: 4 servings.

Per Serving: Calories 171 (39% from fat) Fat 7.4g (sat 1.4g) Protein 14.9g
Carbohydrate 12.9g Fiber 2.9g Cholesterol 5mg Sodium 579mg
Exchanges: 2 Vegetable, 2 Lean Meat

· · · · ·

PARMESAN TOASTS

total time: 6 minutes

Coat 4 slices Italian bread with olive oil-flavored cooking spray; sprinkle evenly with ¼ teaspoon freshly ground black pepper. Top each slice with 1 teaspoon grated Parmesan cheese, and broil 3½ inches from heat until lightly browned.
Yield: 4 servings.

Per Serving: Calories 93 (10% from fat) Fat 1.0g (sat 0.3g) Protein 3.4g
Carbohydrate 17.1g Fiber 0.8g Cholesterol 2mg Sodium 207mg
Exchange: 1 Starch

Grocery List

2 (8-ounce) packages
European-style mixed
salad greens

2 pints cherry tomatoes
(20 tomatoes)

1 pound green grapes

1 loaf
sliced Italian bread

1 bottle fat-free
raspberry vinaigrette

1 (8-ounce) can grated
Parmesan cheese

1 (4-ounce) package
crumbled blue cheese

½ pound sliced deli
roast beef

Great no-cook salad.

Serve with Parmesan Toasts and green grapes.

BEEF AND BLACK BEAN CHILI

total time: 15 minutes

1   pound ground round
2   (15-ounce) cans no-salt-added black beans, undrained
1   cup medium or hot chunky salsa
2   (8-ounce) cans no-salt-added tomato sauce
1   tablespoon chili seasoning mix
Low-fat sour cream (optional)
Shredded reduced-fat Cheddar cheese (optional)

Cook meat in a large saucepan over medium-high heat until meat is browned, stirring until it crumbles. Drain, if necessary.

While meat cooks, drain and mash 1 can of beans. Add mashed beans, undrained beans, salsa, tomato sauce, and seasoning mix to saucepan; stir well. Cook over medium heat 10 minutes or until thoroughly heated.

Spoon into serving bowls. If desired, top with sour cream and shredded cheese.

Yield: 7 (1-cup) servings.

Per Serving: Calories 236 (15% from fat)   Fat 3.9g (sat 1.3g)   Protein 22.8g
Carbohydrate 27.6g   Fiber 5.2g   Cholesterol 38mg   Sodium 229mg
Exchanges: 2 Starch, 2 Lean Meat

A bowl of weeknight comfort.

Enjoy your chili with low-fat tortilla chips
and fresh pineapple slices.

Grocery List

6 oranges

1 medium onion

1 (15-ounce) can low-fat
chili beef soup

1 (11-ounce) can
Mexican-style corn

1 (6-ounce) package
buttermilk cornbread mix

1 (8-ounce) package
shredded reduced-fat
Mexican blend cheese

CHILI-CORNBREAD PIE

work time: 10 minutes • cook time: 18 minutes

Cooking spray
1   medium onion, chopped
1   (15-ounce) can low-fat chili beef soup
1   (11-ounce) can Mexican-style corn, drained
1   cup (4 ounces) shredded reduced-fat Mexican blend cheese
1   (6-ounce) package buttermilk cornbread mix
⅔   cup water

Preheat oven to 450°.

Coat a nonstick skillet with cooking spray; place over medium-high heat until hot. Add onion, and sauté until tender.

Add soup and corn to skillet, stirring well; spoon mixture into an 8-inch square baking dish coated with cooking spray. Sprinkle cheese over soup mixture.

Combine cornbread mix and water, stirring just until smooth. Pour batter over mixture in baking dish; bake at 450° for 18 minutes or until golden.

Yield: 6 servings.

Per Serving: Calories 270 (24% from fat)   Fat 7.3g (sat 2.7g)   Protein 13.7g
Carbohydrate 39.5g   Fiber 3.5g   Cholesterol 13mg   Sodium 798mg
Exchanges: 2 Starch, 1 Vegetable, 1 High-Fat Meat

Saucy chili with crumbled cornbread,
all in one pan. Slice sweet, juicy oranges for dessert.

DEEP-DISH PIZZA CASSEROLE

work time: 10 minutes • cook time: 17 minutes

Grocery List

1 (10-ounce) package
mixed salad greens

1 (15-ounce) can chunky
Italian-style tomato sauce

1 bottle low-fat
vinaigrette

1 (10-ounce) can
refrigerated
pizza crust dough

1 (8-ounce) package
sliced part-skim
mozzarella cheese

1 pound
ground round

1   **pound ground round**
1   **(15-ounce) can chunky Italian-style tomato sauce**
Cooking spray
1   **(10-ounce) can refrigerated pizza crust dough**
6   **(1-ounce) slices part-skim mozzarella cheese, divided**

Cook meat in a medium nonstick skillet over medium-high heat until browned, stirring until it crumbles. Drain, if necessary and return to skillet. Add tomato sauce, and cook until heated.

While meat cooks, coat a 13- x 9- x 2-inch baking dish with cooking spray. Unroll pizza crust dough, and press into bottom and halfway up sides of baking dish. Line bottom of pizza crust with 3 slices mozzarella cheese. Top with meat mixture.

Bake, uncovered, at 425° for 12 minutes. Top with remaining 3 cheese slices, and bake 5 additional minutes or until crust is browned and cheese melts. Cool 5 minutes before serving.

Yield: 6 servings.

Per Serving: Calories 277 (25% from fat)   Fat 7.7g (sat 2.1g)   Protein 22.6g
Carbohydrate 28.5g   Fiber 1.6g   Cholesterol 49mg   Sodium 667mg
Exchanges: 2 Starch, 2 Lean Meat

A meaty, cheesy pizza in a casserole dish.

It's great with a big tossed green salad.

GROUND BEEF STROGANOFF

total time: 14 minutes

8   ounces wide egg noodles, uncooked
1   pound ground round
3   green onions, sliced or 1 cup chopped onion
1   (8-ounce) package sliced fresh mushrooms
1   (12-ounce) jar fat-free beef gravy
1   (8-ounce) carton fat-free sour cream
¼   teaspoon garlic salt
¼   teaspoon freshly ground pepper
1   tablespoon dry sherry (optional)

Prepare noodles according to package directions, omitting salt and fat.
While noodles cook, cook meat, green onions and mushrooms in a
large nonstick skillet until meat is browned, stirring until it crumbles;
drain.
Return meat mixture to skillet; add gravy and next 3 ingredients, stirring well. Cook over medium heat 3 to 5 minutes or until thoroughly
heated. Stir in sherry, if desired. Serve over drained noodles.
Yield: 5 servings.

Per Serving: Calories 367 (19% from fat)   Fat 7.6g (sat 2.4g)   Protein 31.1g
Carbohydrate 42.9g   Fiber 3.9g   Cholesterol 98mg   Sodium 611mg
Exchanges: 3 Starch, 3 Lean Meat

Grocery List

3 green onions or
1 medium onion

1 (8-ounce) package
sliced fresh mushrooms

5 dinner rolls

1 (12-ounce) jar fat-free
beef gravy

Garlic salt

Dry sherry (optional)

1 (8-ounce) package
wide egg noodles

1 (8-ounce) carton
fat-free sour cream

2 (10-ounce) packages
frozen English peas

1 pound ground round

Comfort food with all the flavor

…but not the fat. Heat up some English peas

and rolls to go with the hearty beef and noodles.

BARBECUE MEAT LOAF

work time: 8 minutes • cook time: 25 minutes

Grocery List

1 (16-ounce) package
baby carrots

Barbecue sauce

Garlic powder

1 (15-ounce) container
Italian-seasoned dry
breadcrumbs

Fat-free milk

1 (10-ounce) package
frozen chopped onion

1 (22-ounce) package
frozen mashed potatoes

2 eggs

1 pound
ground round

1   **pound ground round**
½   **cup barbecue sauce, divided**
¼   **cup frozen chopped onion, pressed dry**
¼   **cup Italian-seasoned dry breadcrumbs**
2   **egg whites**
¼   **teaspoon pepper**

Combine meat, ¼ cup barbecue sauce, onion, breadcrumbs, egg whites, and pepper in a large bowl; stir well.

Shape mixture into a 7- x 5-inch loaf on a rack in a roasting pan. Spread remaining ¼ cup barbecue sauce over loaf. Bake at 375° for 25 minutes or to desired degree of doneness.

Yield: 4 servings.

Per Serving: Calories 228 (30% from fat)   Fat 7.6g (sat 2.6g)   Protein 27.7g
Carbohydrate 10.4g   Fiber 0.5g   Cholesterol 70mg   Sodium 535mg
Exchanges: 1 Starch, 3 Lean Meat

• • • • •

GARLIC MASHED POTATOES

total time: 10 minutes

While meat loaf bakes, combine 2⅔ cups frozen mashed potatoes (one-half of a 22-ounce package), 1⅓ cups fat-free milk, ¼ teaspoon salt, ¼ teaspoon pepper, and ¼ teaspoon garlic powder in a 1½-quart baking dish. Cook according to package microwave directions.

Yield: 4 servings.

Per Serving: Calories 120 (20% from fat)   Fat 2.7g (sat 0.1g)   Protein 4.8g
Carbohydrate 20.2g   Fiber 1.0g   Cholesterol 4mg   Sodium 339mg
Exchanges: 1½ Starch

Meat loaf and mashed potatoes—
just like home.

Add steamed carrots. Your mom will be pleased.

BEEF STIR-FRY WITH OYSTER SAUCE

total time: 16 minutes

1   large bag boil-in-bag rice
1   pound boneless top sirloin
Cooking spray
1   teaspoon minced garlic
1   (16-ounce) package frozen broccoli stir-fry vegetables, thawed
¼   cup oyster sauce or Worcestershire sauce

Prepare rice according to package directions, omitting salt and fat, to make 3 cups cooked rice.

While rice cooks, slice meat across grain into very thin strips. Coat a wok or large nonstick skillet with cooking spray; heat at medium-high (375°) until hot. Add meat and garlic; stir-fry until browned.

Add broccoli stir-fry vegetables and oyster sauce to skillet; stir-fry 5 minutes or until thoroughly heated. Serve over rice.

Yield: 4 servings.

Per Serving: Calories 366 (15% from fat)   Fat 6.0g (sat 2.1g)   Protein 29.6g
Carbohydrate 47.9g   Fiber 3.4g   Cholesterol 69mg   Sodium 345mg
Exchanges: 3 Starch, 1 Vegetable, 3 Lean Meat

Grocery List

1 (4½-ounce) jar minced garlic

Oyster sauce or Worcestershire sauce

1 box family-size boil-in-bag rice

1 (16-ounce) package frozen broccoli stir-fry vegetables

1 pound boneless top sirloin

Better than takeout
...and quicker!
Whip up a **Raspberry Smoothie** (page 225)
to finish the meal.

Pan-Seared Steaks with Roasted Red Pepper Sauce

total time: 10 minutes

1   teaspoon roasted garlic-pepper seasoning or ½ teaspoon black
        pepper and ½ teaspoon garlic powder
½   teaspoon salt, divided
4   (4-ounce) lean, boneless beef tenderloin steaks (1 inch thick)
Olive oil-flavored cooking spray
1   (7-ounce) jar roasted red peppers in water, drained

Combine garlic pepper and ¼ teaspoon salt. Rub both sides of steaks
with pepper mixture.

Place a large nonstick skillet coated with cooking spray over medium-high
heat until hot. Add steaks; cook 2 to 3 minutes on each side or until done.

While steaks cook, place peppers and remaining ¼ teaspoon salt in
container of an electric blender. Cover and process until smooth. Serve
steaks with roasted red pepper sauce.

Yield: 4 servings.

Per Serving: Calories 188 (38% from fat)   Fat 8.0g (sat 3.1g)   Protein 24.6g
Carbohydrate 3.4g   Fiber 0.1g   Cholesterol 71mg   Sodium 379mg
Exchanges: 1 Vegetable, 3 Lean Meat

· · · · ·

Baked Potatoes

total time: 12 minutes

Scrub 4 (6-ounce) baking potatoes; pierce each potato several times
with a fork. Microwave at HIGH 12 minutes or until done, rearranging
once. Top each potato with ½ tablespoon reduced-fat margarine, and
sprinkle with pepper, if desired.

Yield: 4 servings.

Per Serving: Calories 156 (22% from fat)   Fat 3.8g (sat 0.5g)   Protein 3.7g
Carbohydrate 28.2g   Fiber 2.7g   Cholesterol 0mg   Sodium 67mg
Exchanges: 2 Starch, 1 Fat

Grocery List

4 (6-ounce) baking
potatoes

1 (10-ounce) package
mixed salad greens

1 bottle low-fat
salad dressing

1 (7-ounce) jar roasted
red peppers in water

Roasted garlic-pepper
seasoning
or garlic powder

Reduced-fat
margarine

4 (4-ounce) lean,
boneless beef tenderloin
steaks (1 inch thick)

Your favorite steakhouse meal comes home—
steak, baked potato, salad. Don't forget the dessert:
Brownie Torte (page 223).

Tex-Mex Pepper Steak

total time: 14 minutes

2   regular-size bags boil-in-bag rice
¾   pound flank steak
2   teaspoons chili powder
1   teaspoon ground cumin
¼   teaspoon salt
Cooking spray
1   (16-ounce) package frozen pepper stir-fry
1   (14½-ounce) can Mexican-style tomatoes, undrained

Prepare rice according to package directions, omitting salt and fat, to make 4 cups cooked rice.

While rice cooks, slice steak in half lengthwise; slice each half diagonally across grain into ¼-inch-thick slices. Combine chili powder, cumin, and salt in a zip-top plastic bag; add meat. Seal bag, and shake until meat is well coated.

Coat a large nonstick skillet with cooking spray; place over medium-high heat until hot. Add meat; stir-fry 4 minutes or until browned.

Remove meat from skillet, and set aside; wipe drippings from skillet with a paper towel. Coat skillet with cooking spray; place over medium heat until hot. Add pepper stir-fry; stir-fry 2 minutes or just until tender. Add tomatoes; bring to a boil. Cook 2 minutes, stirring occasionally. Return meat to skillet; cook until thoroughly heated. Remove skillet from heat.

Place 1 cup rice on each of 4 plates; top evenly with meat mixture.

Yield: 4 servings.

Per Serving: Calories 437 (22% from fat)   Fat 10.9g (sat 4.2g)   Protein 22.4g
Carbohydrate 61.6g   Fiber 3.7g   Cholesterol 45mg   Sodium 478mg
Exchanges: 3 Starch, 3 Vegetable, 1 High-Fat Meat

Grocery List

1 (14½-ounce) can
Mexican-style tomatoes

Chili powder

Ground cumin

1 jar fat-free
caramel topping

1 box boil-in-bag rice

1 package 8-inch
flour tortillas

1 (16-ounce) package
frozen pepper stir-fry

½ gallon vanilla
fat-free ice cream

¾ pound flank steak

Wrap up the juicy meat mixture in a
soft flour tortilla … then treat your tastebuds
to vanilla fat-free ice cream with caramel topping.

LAMB CHOPS WITH MINTED SOUR CREAM SAUCE

total time: 16 minutes

Grocery List

1 lemon

1 (16-ounce) package
baby carrots

1 pint fresh strawberries

2 sourdough rolls

Roasted garlic-pepper
seasoning
or garlic powder

Dried mint leaves

1 (10-ounce)
angel food cake

1 (8-ounce) carton
fat-free sour cream

4 (4-ounce) lean
lamb loin chops
(1 inch thick)

¼ cup fat-free sour cream
⅛ teaspoon salt
½ teaspoon dried mint leaves
4 (4-ounce) lean lamb loin chops (1 inch thick)
¼ teaspoon salt
¼ teaspoon roasted garlic-pepper seasoning or
        ⅛ teaspoon black pepper and ⅛ teaspoon garlic powder
Cooking spray

Combine first 3 ingredients; stir well, and set aside.

Trim fat from chops; sprinkle chops with ¼ teaspoon salt and garlic pepper.

Coat a large nonstick skillet with cooking spray; place over medium-high heat until hot. Add chops. Cook 3 to 4 minutes on each side or until browned. Reduce heat to medium-low; cook 2 to 3 additional minutes on each side or to desired degree of doneness. Serve with sour cream sauce.

Yield: 2 servings (serving size: 2 lamb chops).

Per Serving: Calories 267 (38% from fat)   Fat 11.3g (sat 4.0g)   Protein 36.0g
Carbohydrate 2.0g   Fiber 0.0g   Cholesterol 108mg   Sodium 549mg
Exchanges: 5 Lean Meat

· · · · ·

LEMON CARROTS

total time: 6 minutes

Combine one-half of a 16-ounce package baby carrots, ¼ cup water, and 2 teaspoons lemon juice in a 1-quart microwave-safe dish; cover. Microwave at HIGH 7 minutes or until carrots are tender. Sprinkle with lemon zest, if desired.

Yield: 2 (¾-cup) servings.

Per Serving: Calories 50 (4% from fat)   Fat 0.2g (sat 0.0g)   Protein 1.2g
Carbohydrate 11.9g   Fiber 3.6g   Cholesterol 0mg   Sodium 40mg
Exchanges: 2 Vegetable

An impressive dinner menu: lamb chops, baby carrots, and sourdough rolls. Offer angel food cake with strawberries for dessert.

A super-easy marinade infuses the lamb with great flavor while you're at work.

Speedy sides are Summer Squash Medley and couscous.

GRILLED TERIYAKI LAMB CHOPS

work time: 3 minutes • marinate: 8 hours • cook time: 16 minutes

4   (5-ounce) lean lamb loin chops (1½ inches thick)
½ cup chopped onion
½ cup low-sodium teriyaki sauce
1   teaspoon minced garlic
Cooking spray

Trim fat from chops; place chops in a heavy-duty, zip-top plastic bag.
Add onion, teriyaki sauce, and garlic to bag. Seal bag, and marinate
in refrigerator at least 8 hours, turning bag occasionally.
Remove chops from marinade, reserving marinade. Place marinade in
a small saucepan; bring to a boil. Remove from heat, and set aside.
Coat grill rack with cooking spray; place on grill over medium-hot coals
(350° to 400°). Place chops on rack; grill, covered, 8 minutes on each side
or to desired degree of doneness, basting occasionally with marinade.
Yield: 4 servings.

Per Serving: Calories 192 (33% from fat)   Fat 7.0g (sat 2.5g)   Protein 22.4g
Carbohydrate 8.0g   Fiber 0.4g   Cholesterol 67mg   Sodium 700mg
Exchanges: ½ Starch, 3 Lean Meat

• • • • •

SUMMER SQUASH MEDLEY

total time: 7 minutes

Cut 2 yellow squash and 2 zucchini crosswise into ¼-inch-thick slices.
Cook in a large skillet in a small amount of boiling water 3 to 5 minutes
or until crisp-tender; drain. Add ½ teaspoon grated lemon rind, 1
tablespoon lemon juice, 1 teaspoon dried dillweed, and ¼ teaspoon
salt, and toss.
Yield: 4 (¾-cup) servings.

Per Serving: Calories 24 (8% from fat)   Fat 0.2g (sat 0.1g)   Protein 1.6g
Carbohydrate 5.3g   Fiber 1.4g   Cholesterol 0mg   Sodium 151mg
Exchange: 1 Vegetable

Grocery List

1 lemon

2 yellow squash

2 zucchini

1 medium onion

Low-sodium teriyaki
sauce

1 (4½-ounce) jar
minced garlic

Dried dillweed

1 (10-ounce) package
COUSCOUS

4 (5-ounce)
lean lamb loin chops
(1½ inches thick)

GLAZED PORK CHOPS

total time: 17 minutes

Grocery List

1 small onion

1 pound fresh
green beans

4 French rolls

Dijon mustard

Currant jelly

Ground sage

4 (4-ounce) boneless
center-cut pork loin
chops (½ inch thick)

4   (4-ounce) boneless center-cut pork loin chops (½ inch thick)
Cooking spray
⅛   teaspoon ground sage
½   teaspoon salt
¼   teaspoon pepper
¼   cup minced onion
¼   cup currant jelly
1½ teaspoons Dijon mustard

Trim fat from chops. Coat a large nonstick skillet with cooking spray; place over high heat until hot. Sprinkle chops with sage, salt, and pepper; add to skillet, and cook 1 minute on each side. Reduce heat to medium; cook chops 4 to 5 additional minutes on each side or until done. Transfer chops to a serving platter; keep warm.

Add onion to skillet; cook over medium heat 2 minutes, stirring often. Reduce heat; add jelly and mustard, and simmer 2 minutes or until glaze is reduced to ¼ cup. To serve, spoon glaze over chops.

Yield: 4 servings.

Per Serving: Calories 239 (32% from fat)   Fat 8.4g (sat 2.8g)   Protein 25.2g
Carbohydrate 14.4g   Fiber 0.3g   Cholesterol 71mg   Sodium 431mg
Exchanges: 1 Starch, 3 Lean Meat

Great menu if company's coming:

sweet, tangy pork chops, steamed green beans,

and French rolls. For a no-stress dessert,

try the **Raspberry Trifle** on page 224.

Wonderful summertime flavors... peaches, green beans, and tomatoes. Bake reduced-fat biscuits, and scoop up strawberry low-fat frozen yogurt for dessert.

PORK CHOPS WITH PEACHY MUSTARD SAUCE

total time: 14 minutes

4   (4-ounce) boneless center-cut pork loin chops (½ inch thick)
¼   teaspoon salt
¼   teaspoon pepper
Cooking spray
½   cup peach preserves
2   tablespoons Dijon mustard
1   tablespoon water

Trim fat from chops. Sprinkle chops with salt and pepper. Coat a large nonstick skillet with cooking spray, and place over medium-high heat until hot. Add chops to skillet; cook 1 minute on each side. Reduce heat to medium; cook 4 to 6 additional minutes on each side or until done. Remove chops from skillet, and keep warm.

Add peach preserves, mustard, and water to skillet; cook, stirring constantly, 2 minutes. Spoon sauce over chops.

Yield: 4 servings.

Per Serving: Calories 287 (27% from fat)   Fat 8.7g (sat 2.8g)   Protein 25.2g   Carbohydrate 26.3g   Fiber 0.5g   Cholesterol 71mg   Sodium 460mg
Exchanges: 1½ Starch, 3 Lean Meat

• • • • •

SKILLET BEANS AND TOMATOES

total time: 12 minutes

Combine 1 (10-ounce) package frozen cut green beans, ½ cup coarsely chopped onion, 1 teaspoon sugar, ¼ teaspoon salt, and ¼ teaspoon pepper in a large nonstick skillet coated with cooking spray. Cover and cook 8 minutes, stirring occasionally. Add 2 medium tomatoes, cut into chunks; cover and cook 2 minutes or until thoroughly heated.

Yield: 4 (¾-cup) servings.

Per Serving: Calories 47 (8% from fat)   Fat 0.4g (sat 0.0g)   Protein 2.0g   Carbohydrate 10.5g   Fiber 1.2g   Cholesterol 0mg   Sodium 162mg
Exchanges: 2 Vegetable

Grocery List

2 medium-size tomatoes

1 medium onion

Dijon mustard

Peach preserves

Sugar

1 (10.2-ounce) can refrigerated reduced-fat biscuits

½ gallon strawberry low-fat frozen yogurt

1 (10-ounce) package frozen cut green beans

4 (4-ounce) boneless center-cut pork loin chops (½ inch thick)

SKILLET CHOPS AND RICE

total time: 15 minutes

4 (6-ounce) center-cut pork chops (½ inch thick)
Cooking spray
1½ cups quick-cooking 5-minute rice, uncooked
⅔ cup water
½ cup chopped onion
¼ teaspoon pepper
1 (14½-ounce) can Italian-style stewed tomatoes, undrained and chopped
1 (8-ounce) can no-salt-added tomato sauce

Trim fat from chops. Coat a large nonstick skillet with cooking spray, and place over medium-high heat until hot. Add chops, and cook 2 minutes on each side. Remove from skillet; set aside.

Combine rice and remaining 5 ingredients in skillet; bring to a boil. Arrange chops over rice mixture. Cover, reduce heat, and cook 5 minutes or until liquid is absorbed and rice is done.

Yield: 4 servings.

Per Serving: Calories 375 (20% from fat) Fat 8.5g (sat 2.9g) Protein 29.5g
Carbohydrate 42.9g Fiber 2.2g Cholesterol 71mg Sodium 352mg
Exchanges: 2 Starch, 2 Vegetable, 3 Lean Meat

A simple, one-skillet supper. Good with steamed lima beans. Treat the kids (or the kid in you) to **Ice Cream Sandwiches** (page 223) for dessert.

Grocery List

1 medium onion

1 (14½-ounce) can
Italian-style stewed
tomatoes

1 (8-ounce) can
no-salt-added
tomato sauce

1 (14-ounce) box
quick-cooking 5-minute
rice (such as Uncle Ben's
Instant)

1 (16-ounce) package
frozen lima beans

4 (6-ounce) center-cut
pork chops
(½ inch thick)

BALSAMIC PORK CHOPS

total time: 16 minutes

4   (4-ounce) boneless center-cut pork loin chops (½ inch thick)
1   teaspoon salt-free lemon-herb seasoning
Cooking spray
½   cup balsamic vinegar
⅓   cup fat-free, reduced-sodium chicken broth

Trim fat from chops. Sprinkle chops evenly on both sides with season-ing. Coat a medium nonstick skillet with cooking spray; place over medium-high heat until hot. Add chops, and cook 3 to 4 minutes on each side or until lightly browned. Remove chops from skillet, and keep warm.

Wipe drippings from skillet with a paper towel. Combine vinegar and broth in skillet. Cook over medium-high heat until mixture is reduced to a thin sauce (about 5 to 6 minutes), stirring occasionally. Spoon sauce over chops.
Yield: 4 servings.

Per Serving: Calories 210 (49% from fat)   Fat 11.4g (sat 3.8g)   Protein 24.3g
Carbohydrate 0.9g   Fiber 0.1g   Cholesterol 77mg   Sodium 178mg
Exchanges: 3 Lean Meat

· · · · ·

ROASTED ASPARAGUS

total time: 12 minutes

Snap tough ends off 1 pound fresh asparagus. Coat asparagus with olive oil-flavored cooking spray, and bake at 450° for 10 minutes or until tender.
Yield: 4 servings.

Per Serving: Calories 18 (25% from fat)   Fat 0.5g (sat 0.0g)   Protein 1.5g
Carbohydrate 2.9g   Fiber 1.3g   Cholesterol 0mg   Sodium 1mg
Exchange: 1 Vegetable

One of the most flavorful pork chops you'll ever eat.

Roasted Asparagus and nutty couscous complement the rich balsamic sauce.

It's hard to believe the thick, creamy sauce on the chops is fat-free—so are the potatoes and the broccoli spears. So reward yourself with dessert: Try **Frozen Chocolate Pie** (page 223).

PORK CHOPS WITH DIJON CREAM SAUCE

total time: 15 minutes

4   (4-ounce) boneless center-cut pork loin chops (½ inch thick)
½   teaspoon salt
½   teaspoon coarsely ground pepper
Cooking spray
⅓   cup fat-free, reduced-sodium chicken broth
1½   tablespoons Dijon mustard
⅓   cup fat-free half-and-half or fat-free evaporated milk

Trim fat from chops. Sprinkle both sides of chops evenly with salt and pepper. Coat a large nonstick skillet with cooking spray; place over medium-high heat until hot. Add chops to skillet, and cook 3 to 4 minutes on each side or until browned. Remove chops from skillet, and keep warm.

Add broth to skillet, stirring to loosen browned bits. Combine mustard and half-and-half; add to skillet. Reduce heat, and simmer 7 minutes or until sauce is thickened slightly. Spoon sauce over chops.

Yield: 4 servings.

Per Serving: Calories 201 (40% from fat)   Fat 9.0g (sat 3.0g)   Protein 23.5g
Carbohydrate 2.7g   Fiber 0.1g   Cholesterol 68mg   Sodium 567mg
Exchanges: 3 Lean Meat

. . . . .

STEAMED POTATOES

total time: 10 minutes

Quarter 1 pound round red potatoes, and place in a microwave-safe dish. Add 2 tablespoons water, and cover. Microwave at HIGH 8 minutes or until tender. Coat with butter-flavored spray, and sprinkle with ¼ teaspoon salt and ¼ teaspoon pepper.

Yield: 4 servings.

Per Serving: Calories 86 (3% from fat)   Fat 0.3g (sat 0.0g)   Protein 2.5g
Carbohydrate 18.9g   Fiber 2.1g   Cholesterol 0mg   Sodium 155mg
Exchange: 1 Starch

Grocery List

1 pound
round red potatoes

1 (14¼-ounce) can
fat-free, reduced-sodium
chicken broth

Dijon mustard

1 pint fat-free half-and-
half or 1 can fat-free
evaporated milk

Butter-flavored spray
(such as "I Can't Believe
It's Not Butter")

2 (10-ounce) packages
frozen broccoli spears

4 (4-ounce) boneless
center-cut pork loin
chops (½ inch thick)

HONEY-MUSTARD PORK WITH WILTED SPINACH

total time: 15 minutes

1   (1½-pound) honey-mustard-flavored pork tenderloin
¼   teaspoon pepper
Cooking spray
3   tablespoons lemon juice
4   green onions, finely chopped
1   (16-ounce) package frozen leaf spinach, thawed and drained

Trim fat from pork, and cut tenderloin crosswise into 1-inch-thick pieces. Sprinkle with pepper. Coat a large nonstick skillet with cooking spray, and place over medium-high heat until hot. Add pork; cook 3 minutes on each side. Remove pork, reserving drippings in skillet. Set pork aside, and keep warm.

Add lemon juice and green onions to skillet; stir in spinach. Cook, stirring constantly, 3 minutes, or until thoroughly heated. Arrange spinach evenly on plates. Top evenly with pork.

Yield: 6 servings.

Per Serving: Calories 166 (29% from fat)   Fat 5.3g (sat 2.0g)   Protein 22.5g
Carbohydrate 5.1g   Fiber 2.6g   Cholesterol 55mg   Sodium 456mg
Exchanges: 1 Vegetable, 3 Very Lean Meat

• • • • •

CRANBERRY WALDORF SALAD

total time: 10 minutes

Combine 2 small cored and chopped Red Delicious apples, ¼ cup chopped celery, 1½ tablespoons chopped walnuts, and ⅓ cup cranberry-orange relish in a bowl; toss. Cover and chill.

Yield: 6 servings.

Per Serving: Calories 67 (17% from fat)   Fat 1.3g (sat 0.1g)   Protein 0.6g
Carbohydrate 14.0g   Fiber 1.7g   Cholesterol 0mg   Sodium 6mg
Exchange: 1 Fruit

A nice twist for a quick holiday meal . . .

pork tenderloin, cranberry salad, and whole wheat rolls.

Make the salad first so it can chill.

Round out this
Asian-flavored meal with rice,
steamed snow peas, and orange sherbet.

TERIYAKI-GINGER PORK TENDERLOIN

total time: 14 minutes

1   (1-pound) pork tenderloin
Cooking spray
1½ tablespoons roasted garlic or regular teriyaki sauce
1½ teaspoons cornstarch
¼ teaspoon ground ginger
1   (6-ounce) can pineapple juice

Trim fat from pork. Slice tenderloin into ½-inch thick slices; flatten slices with palm of hand. Coat a large nonstick skillet with cooking spray; place over medium-high heat until hot. Add pork, and cook 3 minutes on each side or until browned.
Combine teriyaki sauce and remaining 3 ingredients, stirring well. Add to pork in skillet. Bring to a boil; reduce heat, and simmer 3 minutes. Remove pork from skillet, and spoon sauce over pork.
Yield: 4 servings.

Per Serving: Calories 161 (17% from fat)   Fat 3.0g (sat 1.0g)   Protein 24.3g
Carbohydrate 7.8g   Fiber 0.1g   Cholesterol 74mg   Sodium 293mg
Exchanges: ½ Starch, 3 Very Lean Meat

· · · · ·

CURRIED RICE

total time: 12 minutes

Prepare 2 cups cooked rice using 1 regular bag boil-in-bag rice. Add ¼ teaspoon salt, ½ teaspoon curry powder, 2 tablespoons raisins, and 2 chopped green onions to cooked rice, and stir.
Yield: 4 (½-cup) servings.

Per Serving: Calories 149 (2% from fat)   Fat 0.4g (sat 0.1g)   Protein 3.0g
Carbohydrate 32.9g   Fiber 0.4g   Cholesterol 0mg   Sodium 539mg
Exchanges: 2 Starch

Grocery List

2 green onions

1 (6-ounce) can pineapple juice

Roasted garlic or regular teriyaki sauce

Curry powder

Ground ginger

1 (1.5-ounce) box raisins

Cornstarch

1 box boil-in-bag rice

2 (6-ounce) packages frozen snow peas

½ gallon orange sherbet

1 (1-pound) pork tenderloin (center-cut pork loin fillet)

APRICOT-GLAZED HAM STEAKS

total time: 13 minutes

Grocery List

1 orange (optional)

1 pound fresh
green beans

1 (14½-ounce) can
mashed sweet potatoes

Apricot spreadable fruit
(such as Polaner's)

Brown sugar

Orange juice

Reduced-calorie
margarine

1 (¾-pound) lean ham

1   (¾-pound) lean ham
Cooking spray
¼   **cup apricot spreadable fruit**
¼   **cup orange juice**
Fresh orange slices (optional)

Slice ham into 4 (3-ounce) slices. Coat a large nonstick skillet with cooking spray; place over medium-high heat until hot. Add ham; cook 2 to 3 minutes on each side or until lightly browned.
Add apricot spread and orange juice to skillet, stirring until spread melts. Reduce heat, and simmer 5 to 6 minutes or until ham is glazed. Garnish with orange slices, if desired.
Yield: 4 servings.

Per Serving: Calories 127 (26% from fat)   Fat 3.6g (sat 1.0g)   Protein 15.2g   Carbohydrate 9.1g   Fiber 0.0g   Cholesterol 40mg   Sodium 856mg
Exchanges: ½ Fruit, 2 Lean Meat

• • • • •

BROWN SUGAR SWEET POTATOES

total time: 6 minutes

Combine 1 (14½-ounce) can mashed sweet potatoes, 2 tablespoons brown sugar, 1 tablespoon reduced-calorie margarine, 2 tablespoons orange juice, and ¼ teaspoon salt in a medium saucepan. Cook over medium heat 5 minutes or until smooth and thoroughly heated, stirring often. Stir in 2 to 3 tablespoons water, if necessary.
Yield: 4 (½-cup) servings.

Per Serving: Calories 144 (13% from fat)   Fat 2.1g (sat 0.3g)   Protein 1.7g   Carbohydrate 30.2g   Fiber 3.1g   Cholesterol 0mg   Sodium 189mg
Exchanges: 2 Starch

A saucy, glazed ham that's too easy to be true. And what's better with ham than sweet potatoes and steamed green beans?

Pan-Glazed Chicken with Basil, page 147

In a recent survey, 74% of the people claimed they can judge someone's personality by looking in their refrigerator.

Poultry

To have chicken (or turkey) in your pot every week, keep these speedy items on hand:

- frozen diced cooked chicken breast

- chicken breast tenders

- skinned, boned chicken breast halves

- deli-style turkey breast

- turkey cutlets

- ground turkey

CREAMY CHICKEN-SPINACH SOUP

total time: 14 minutes

1   (9-ounce) package refrigerated cheese tortellini
1   (14¼-ounce) can fat-free, reduced-sodium chicken broth
2   (10¾-ounce) cans reduced-fat, reduced-sodium cream of
       chicken soup
1   (10-ounce) package frozen chopped spinach, thawed
1   (9-ounce) package frozen cooked diced chicken breast
2   cups fat-free milk
½   teaspoon dried thyme
¼   teaspoon pepper

Cook tortellini in a Dutch oven according to package directions, using
1 can broth instead of water. Add soup and remaining ingredients,
stirring well.
Bring to a boil; cover, reduce heat to medium, and cook until
thoroughly heated.
Yield: 6 (1⅓-cup) servings.

Per Serving: Calories 300 (21% from fat)   Fat 7.0g (sat 3.1g)   Protein 24.7g
Carbohydrate 35.0g   Fiber 2.6g   Cholesterol 68mg   Sodium 759mg
Exchanges: 2 Starch, 1 Vegetable, 2 Lean Meat

A quick weeknight meal.

Savor this creamy, chunky soup with

thick slices of whole wheat bread.

Grocery List

1 loaf whole wheat bread

1 (14¼-ounce) can
fat-free, reduced-sodium
chicken broth

2 (10¾-ounce) cans
reduced-fat, reduced-
sodium cream of chicken
soup

Dried thyme

1 (9-ounce) package
refrigerated cheese
tortellini

Fat-free milk

1 (10-ounce) package
frozen chopped spinach

1 (9-ounce) package
frozen cooked diced
chicken breast

WAGON WHEEL PASTA WITH SALSA CHICKEN

total time: 13 minutes

8   ounces wagon wheel pasta, uncooked
1   (24-ounce) jar thick and chunky mild salsa
1   (9-ounce) package frozen cooked diced chicken breast
½   cup (2 ounces) shredded reduced-fat Monterey Jack cheese

Cook pasta according to package directions, omitting salt and fat.
While pasta cooks, combine salsa and chicken in a medium nonstick skillet. Cover and cook over medium heat 5 minutes or until chicken is thoroughly heated, stirring occasionally.
Place 1 cup drained pasta on each of 4 plates; top evenly with chicken mixture and cheese.
Yield: 4 servings.

Per Serving: Calories 395 (14% from fat)   Fat 6.2g (sat 2.4g)   Protein 33.1g
Carbohydrate 51.0g   Fiber 4.6g   Cholesterol 64mg   Sodium 647mg
Exchanges: 3 Starch, 1 Vegetable, 3 Lean Meat

•   •   •   •   •

BERRIES AND CREAM

total time: 5 minutes

Combine 2 cups each fresh blueberries and fresh strawberry halves; spoon evenly into 4 dessert dishes. Combine ½ cup vanilla low-fat yogurt and 1½ tablespoons honey; spoon evenly over fruit mixture.
Yield: 4 (1-cup) servings.

Per Serving: Calories 111 (7% from fat)   Fat 0.9g (sat 0.3g)   Protein 2.4g
Carbohydrate 26.0g   Fiber 5.2g   Cholesterol 1mg   Sodium 24mg
Exchanges: 2 Fruit

You can't miss with this one-dish meal

of chicken, pasta, and melted cheese. Berries and

Cream is a cool finish for the spicy chicken.

1 medium cantaloupe

6 French rolls

1 (15-ounce) can low-fat chicken alfredo-style soup

Raspberry wine vinegar

Honey

1 jar poppy seeds

1 (8-ounce) package rotini

1 (8-ounce) can grated Parmesan cheese

1 (10-ounce) package frozen mixed vegetables

1 (9-ounce) package frozen cooked diced chicken breast

Hard to believe this creamy pasta is low-fat. Serve it with the cantaloupe salad and warm rolls.

CHICKEN ALFREDO PASTA

total time: 15 minutes

5½ ounces rotini, uncooked (2 cups)
1   (10-ounce) package frozen mixed vegetables
1   (9-ounce) package frozen cooked diced chicken breast
1   (15-ounce) can low-fat chicken alfredo-style soup
¼   cup grated Parmesan cheese
½   teaspoon salt
¼   teaspoon freshly ground pepper

Cook pasta and vegetables together in boiling water in a Dutch oven
10 minutes or until pasta is done and vegetables are tender.
Drain pasta and vegetables; return to Dutch oven. Add chicken and
next 3 ingredients to pasta mixture, stirring well. Cook over low heat 2
minutes or until thoroughly heated. Sprinkle with freshly ground pepper.
Yield: 6 (1-cup) servings.

Per Serving: Calories 253 (14% from fat)   Fat 3.8g (sat 1.5g)   Protein 22.4g
Carbohydrate 31.5g   Fiber 2.8g   Cholesterol 42mg   Sodium 516mg
Exchanges: 2 Starch, 2 Lean Meat

• • • • •

CANTALOUPE WITH RASPBERRY-POPPY SEED DRESSING

total time: 6 minutes

Cut 1 medium cantaloupe into 6 slices. Combine ¼ cup
raspberry wine vinegar, 1½ tablespoons honey, and 1 teaspoon
poppy seeds, stirring well; drizzle evenly over cantaloupe.
Yield: 6 servings.

Per Serving: Calories 51 (9% from fat)   Fat 0.5g (sat 0.2g)   Protein 0.9g
Carbohydrate 11.9g   Fiber 1.1g   Cholesterol 0mg   Sodium 9mg
Exchange: 1 Fruit

SPEEDY CHICKEN CACCIATORE

total time: 15 minutes

Grocery List

1 medium-size green
pepper

1 small onion

1 loaf French bread

1 (15-ounce) can chunky
Italian-style tomato sauce

1 (9-ounce) package
refrigerated
angel hair pasta

1 (18-ounce) package
frozen cooked diced
chicken breast

1 (9-ounce) package refrigerated angel hair pasta
Olive oil-flavored cooking spray
1 (18-ounce) package frozen cooked diced chicken breast
1 medium-size green pepper, cut into 1-inch pieces (about 1 cup)
1 small onion, cut into 1-inch pieces (about 1 cup)
1 (15-ounce) can chunky Italian-style tomato sauce
⅔ cup water
¼ teaspoon pepper

Cook pasta according to package directions, omitting salt and fat.
While pasta cooks, coat a large nonstick skillet with cooking spray; place over medium-high heat until hot. Add chicken, green pepper, and onion; sauté until chicken is browned and vegetables are crisp-tender. Stir in tomato sauce, water, and ¼ teaspoon pepper. Reduce heat, and simmer, uncovered, 5 minutes, stirring often.
Place ¾ cup drained pasta on each of 4 plates; top each serving with 1 cup chicken mixture.
Yield: 5 servings.

Per Serving: Calories 416 (13% from fat) Fat 6.1g (sat 1.2g) Protein 40.1g
Carbohydrate 47.1g Fiber 3.5g Cholesterol 87mg Sodium 591mg
Exchanges: 3 Starch, 4 Very Lean Meat

A speedy version of an Italian classic.

It's good with a loaf of crusty bread.

Enjoy this spicy one-skillet supper with nacho-flavored tortilla chips and a Mocha Milk Shake for dessert.

MEXICAN CHICKEN SKILLET

total time: 14 minutes

Cooking spray
1   (9-ounce) package frozen Southwestern-flavored cooked chicken
    breast strips
1¾ cups water
1   (14½-ounce) can Mexican-style stewed tomatoes
2   cups instant rice, uncooked
1   (8¾-ounce) can no-salt-added whole-kernel corn, drained
1   cup (4 ounces) shredded reduced-fat Mexican blend cheese

Coat a large nonstick skillet with cooking spray; place over medium-high heat until hot. Add chicken strips, and sauté 3 to 5 minutes or until chicken is thoroughly heated. Remove chicken from skillet, and set aside. **Add** water and tomatoes to skillet; bring to a boil. Stir in rice and corn; top with chicken strips and cheese. Cover, remove from heat, and let stand 5 minutes.
Yield: 4 servings.

Per Serving: 402 Calories (17% from fat)   Fat 7.7g (sat 3.8g)   Protein 27.1g
Carbohydrate 55.5g   Fiber 1.3g   Cholesterol 40mg   Sodium 767mg
Exchanges: 3 Starch, 2 Vegetable, 2 Lean Meat

· · · · ·

MOCHA MILK SHAKE

total time: 5 minutes

Combine 3¼ cups vanilla low-fat ice cream, ¾ cup cold coffee, ¼ cup fat-free hot fudge topping, and 1½ cups ice in container of an electric blender; cover and process until smooth.
Yield: 4 (1-cup) servings.

Per Serving: 195 Calories (21% from fat)   Fat 4.6g (sat 2.8g)   Protein 5.1g
Carbohydrate 36.0g   Fiber 1.0g   Cholesterol 15mg   Sodium 138mg
Exchanges: 2½ Starch, 1 Fat

Grocery List

1 (14½-ounce) can
Mexican-style stewed
tomatoes

1 (8¾-ounce) can
no-salt-added
whole-kernel corn

1 (11.5-ounce) jar
fat-free hot fudge topping

1 (14-ounce) box
instant rice

1 bag low-fat
nacho-flavored
tortilla chips

Coffee

1 (8-ounce) package
shredded reduced-fat
Mexican blend cheese

½ gallon vanilla
low-fat ice cream

1 (9-ounce) package
frozen Southwestern-
flavored cooked chicken
breast strips

Grocery List

1 (10-ounce) package
fresh stir-fry
vegetables

2 green onions

Low-sodium teriyaki
sauce

Low-sodium soy sauce

Dried red pepper flakes

Dark or light sesame oil

1 (5-ounce) package
Japanese curly noodles

1 bag mini rice cakes

1 pound chicken breast
tenders

SZECHUAN CHICKEN AND VEGETABLES

total time: 9 minutes

2   teaspoons dark or light sesame oil
1   pound chicken breast tenders
¼   teaspoon dried red pepper flakes
1   (10-ounce) package fresh stir-fry vegetables (about 2½ cups)
¼   cup low-sodium teriyaki sauce

Heat oil in a large nonstick skillet over medium-high heat. Add chicken, and sprinkle with pepper flakes; stir-fry 3 minutes.
Add vegetables and teriyaki sauce; stir-fry 5 minutes or until vegetables are crisp-tender and chicken is thoroughly cooked.
Yield: 4 servings.

Per Serving: 183 Calories (18% from fat)   Fat 3.7g (sat 0.7g)   Protein 28.8g
Carbohydrate 7.9g   Fiber 1.2g   Cholesterol 66mg   Sodium 341mg
Exchanges: 2 Vegetable, 3 Very Lean Meat

• • • • •

ASIAN NOODLES

total time: 8 minutes

Cook 1 (5-ounce) package Japanese curly noodles according to package directions; drain well. Combine noodles, 2 tablespoons low-sodium soy sauce, 1 teaspoon sesame oil, and ½ cup thinly sliced green onions.
Yield: 4 (¾-cup) servings.

Per Serving: 140 Calories (12% from fat)   Fat 1.8g (sat 0.2g)   Protein 3.9g
Carbohydrate 26.5g   Fiber 0.8g   Cholesterol 0mg   Sodium 389mg
Exchanges: 2 Starch

Start the noodles first, then stir-fry the chicken and vegetables.

Add crunch to the meal with mini rice cakes.

PEACH-GLAZED CHICKEN

total time: 14 minutes

Cooking spray
1 teaspoon vegetable oil
1 pound chicken breast tenders
½ cup peach preserves
2 tablespoons balsamic vinegar
1 green onion, chopped
¼ teaspoon pepper

Coat a large nonstick skillet with cooking spray; add oil, and place over medium-high heat until hot. Add chicken, and sauté 5 minutes on each side or until done. Remove chicken; set aside, and keep warm.
Reduce heat to low; add preserves and remaining 3 ingredients. Cook, stirring constantly, until preserves melt and onion is tender. Spoon preserves mixture over chicken.
Yield: 4 servings.

Per Serving: Calories 238 (10% from fat) Fat 2.7g (sat 0.6g) Protein 26.3g
Carbohydrate 26.4g Fiber 0.1g Cholesterol 66mg Sodium 95mg
Exchanges: 2 Starch, 3 Very Lean Meat

• • • • •

SWEET-AND-SOUR SPINACH SALAD

total time: 8 minutes

Combine 1 (10-ounce) package torn fresh spinach, 1 cup croutons, 2 tablespoons crumbled bacon bits, and ½ cup fat-free sweet-and-sour dressing; toss well.
Yield: 6 (1½-cup) servings.

Per Serving: Calories 77 (17% from fat) Fat 1.5g (sat 0.4g) Protein 2.9g
Carbohydrate 13.5g Fiber 2.1g Cholesterol 2mg Sodium 476mg
Exchange: 1 Starch

Grocery List

1 (10-ounce) package fresh spinach

1 green onion

1 bottle fat-free sweet-and-sour dressing

1 jar crumbled bacon bits

Balsamic vinegar

Peach preserves

Vegetable oil

1 (5.5-ounce) box croutons

1 box boil-in-bag rice

1 pound chicken breast tenders

Pair the saucy glazed chicken

with rice and the tangy spinach salad.

Grocery List

2 green onions

1 (14¼-ounce) can
fat-free, reduced-sodium
chicken broth

Curry powder

Salt-free Moroccan
seasoning
(such as Spice Hunter)

1 (10-ounce) package
couscous

1 (2-ounce) package
chopped walnuts

1 (8-ounce) package
dried apricot halves

Olive oil

1 (8-ounce) carton
reduced-fat sour cream

1 pound chicken breast
tenders

FRUITED MOROCCAN CHICKEN

total time: 9 minutes

1   tablespoon salt-free Moroccan seasoning
1   pound chicken breast tenders
Cooking spray
1   teaspoon olive oil
16 dried apricot halves
½   cup reduced-fat sour cream (do not use fat-free sour cream)

Sprinkle seasoning evenly over chicken. Coat a large nonstick skillet with cooking spray; add oil. Place over medium-high heat until hot. Add chicken; cook 3 minutes on each side or until chicken is lightly browned.

While chicken cooks, cut apricot halves into slivers. Place in a glass measure; add water to cover. Cover with heavy-duty plastic wrap, and vent. Microwave at HIGH 2 minutes; drain well.

Remove chicken from heat; stir in apricots and sour cream. Serve immediately.

Yield: 4 servings.

Per Serving: Calories 233 (25% from fat)   Fat 6.4g (sat 3.0g)   Protein 29.0g Carbohydrate 15.0g   Fiber 0.6g   Cholesterol 81mg   Sodium 110mg **Exchanges:** 1 Fruit, 4 Very Lean Meat, ½ Fat

•   •   •   •   •

CURRIED COUSCOUS WITH WALNUTS

total time: 8 minutes

Combine 1 (14¼-ounce) can fat-free, reduced-sodium chicken broth, ¼ cup water, and ½ teaspoon curry powder in a medium saucepan; bring to a boil. Stir in 1 (10-ounce) package couscous; cover, remove from heat, and let stand 5 minutes. Stir in 2 tablespoons chopped walnuts and ½ cup sliced green onions; fluff couscous with a fork.

Yield: 4 servings.

Per Serving: Calories 272 (10% from fat)   Fat 2.9g (sat 0.1g)   Protein 10.1g Carbohydrate 51.6g   Fiber 3.0g   Cholesterol 0mg   Sodium 92mg **Exchanges:** 2½ Starch, 1 Fruit, ½ Fat

Start the couscous first so it can be steaming
while you cook the chicken.

A rustic Italian meal with wonderful flavor.

Add Garlic-Cheese Breadsticks and a fruit sorbet.

Tuscan Chicken and Beans

total time: 13 minutes

Olive oil-flavored cooking spray
1 pound skinned, boned chicken breasts, cut into 1-inch pieces
1 teaspoon dried rosemary, crushed or 2 teaspoons chopped
     fresh rosemary
¼ teaspoon salt
¼ teaspoon freshly ground pepper
1 cup fat-free, reduced-sodium chicken broth
1 (16-ounce) can cannellini beans, rinsed and drained
2 tablespoons sun-dried tomato sprinkles
Fresh rosemary (optional)

Coat a large nonstick skillet with cooking spray; place over medium heat until hot. Add chicken; sprinkle with rosemary, salt, and pepper. Stir-fry 2 minutes.
Add broth, beans, and tomato sprinkles to skillet; bring to a boil. Reduce heat, and simmer, uncovered, 8 minutes or until chicken is done. Sprinkle with fresh rosemary, if desired.
Yield: 4 servings.

Per Serving: Calories 193 (9% from fat)   Fat 1.9g (sat 0.4g)   Protein 29.8g
Carbohydrate 11.0g   Fiber 3.8g   Cholesterol 66mg   Sodium 586mg
Exchanges: 1 Starch, 4 Very Lean Meat

· · · · ·

Garlic-Cheese Breadsticks

total time: 15 minutes

Combine ¼ cup grated Parmesan cheese and ¼ teaspoon garlic powder. Prepare 1 (11-ounce) can refrigerated soft breadsticks according to package directions, pressing each stick into cheese mixture before baking.
Yield: 8 breadsticks.

Per Breadstick: Calories 122 (21% from fat)   Fat 2.8g (sat 0.5g)   Protein 2.6g
Carbohydrate 19.2g   Fiber 0.5g   Cholesterol 2mg   Sodium 337mg
Exchanges: 1 Starch, ½ Fat

Grocery List

1 (14¼-ounce) can
fat-free, reduced-sodium
chicken broth

1 (16-ounce) can
cannellini beans

Garlic powder

Dried or fresh rosemary

1 (3-ounce) package
sun-dried tomato
sprinkles

1 (8-ounce) can grated
Parmesan cheese

1 (11-ounce) can
refrigerated
soft breadsticks

½ gallon frozen fruit
sorbet

1 pound skinned, boned
chicken breasts

GRILLED CARIBBEAN CHICKEN

total time: 14 minutes

4   (4-ounce) skinned, boned chicken breast halves
2   teaspoons lime juice
1   teaspoon vegetable oil
2   teaspoons jerk seasoning
Cooking spray

Place chicken between 2 sheets of heavy-duty plastic wrap, and flatten to ¼-inch thickness, using a meat mallet or rolling pin.

Combine lime juice and oil; brush over both sides of chicken. Rub both sides of chicken with jerk seasoning.

Coat grill rack with cooking spray; place rack on grill over medium-hot coals (350° to 400°). Place chicken on rack; grill, covered, 5 to 6 minutes on each side or until done.

Yield: 4 servings.

Per Serving: Calories 153 (25% from fat)   Fat 4.2g (sat 1.0g)   Protein 25.9g
Carbohydrate 1.4g   Fiber 0.2g   Cholesterol 70mg   Sodium 97mg
Exchanges: 4 Very Lean Meat

• • • • •

REFRESHING MELON DUO

total time: 10 minutes

Combine 2 cups cubed honeydew melon and 2 cups cubed cantaloupe in a bowl. Combine ¼ cup white balsamic vinegar and 1 teaspoon brown sugar; stir to dissolve. Pour over melon cubes; stir gently to coat. Cover and chill.

Yield: 4 (1-cup) servings.

Per Serving: Calories 62 (4% from fat)   Fat 0.3g (sat 0.2g)   Protein 1.1g
Carbohydrate 15.9g   Fiber 1.7g   Cholesterol 0mg   Sodium 16mg
Exchange: 1 Fruit

Get a taste of the islands with the spicy

grilled chicken, rice, and Refreshing Melon Duo.

Serve the citrus chicken with Herbed Sugar Snap Peas and rolls. Enjoy **Fruited Frozen Yogurt** (page 227) for dessert.

Spiced Orange Chicken

total time: 14 minutes

4   (4-ounce) skinned, boned chicken breast halves
¼   teaspoon salt
¼   teaspoon pepper
Cooking spray
½   cup orange sections in light syrup, drained and coarsely chopped
¼   cup orange juice
3   tablespoons low-sugar orange marmalade
¼   teaspoon ground cinnamon

Place chicken between 2 sheets of heavy-duty plastic wrap, and flatten to ¼-inch thickness, using a meat mallet or rolling pin. Sprinkle with salt and pepper.

Coat a large nonstick skillet with cooking spray; place over medium-high heat until hot. Add chicken; cook 3 to 4 minutes or until lightly browned. Turn chicken, reduce heat to medium-low, and cook 2 to 3 additional minutes or until done.

Add orange sections and remaining ingredients to skillet. Cook 2 to 3 minutes or until orange mixture is thoroughly heated. To serve, spoon orange mixture over chicken.

Yield: 4 servings.

Per Serving: Calories 155 (9% from fat)   Fat 1.6g (sat 0.4g)   Protein 26.4g
Carbohydrate 7.1g   Fiber 0.1g   Cholesterol 66mg   Sodium 227mg
Exchanges: ½ Fruit, 4 Very Lean Meat

• • • • •

Herbed Sugar Snap Peas

total time: 10 minutes

Cook 2 (9-ounce) packages frozen Sugar Snap peas according to package microwave directions. Coat cooked peas with butter-flavored spray, and stir in 1 tablespoon fresh basil or other desired herb.

Yield: 4 servings.

Per Serving: Calories 55 (0% from fat)   Fat 0.0g (sat 0.0g)   Protein 3.4g
Carbohydrate 8.8g   Fiber 1.8g   Cholesterol 0mg   Sodium 77mg
Exchange: 1 Vegetable

Grocery List

Fresh basil
or other fresh herb

4 rolls

Low-sugar
orange marmalade

Ground cinnamon

Butter-flavored spray
(such as "I Can't Believe
It's Not Butter")

1 (26-ounce) jar orange
sections in light syrup

Orange juice

2 (9-ounce) packages
frozen Sugar Snap peas

4 (4-ounce) skinned,
boned chicken breast
halves

Grocery List

Fresh basil

1 (14¼-ounce) can
fat-free, reduced-sodium
chicken broth

Balsamic vinegar

Honey

Olive oil

1 (10-ounce) package
couscous

1 (10-ounce) package
frozen chopped broccoli

4 (4-ounce) skinned,
boned chicken breast
halves

Pan-Glazed Chicken with Basil

total time: 18 minutes

4   (4-ounce) skinned, boned chicken breast halves
½   teaspoon salt
¼   teaspoon freshly ground pepper
2   teaspoons olive oil
2   tablespoons balsamic vinegar
1   tablespoon honey
2   tablespoons chopped fresh basil

Sprinkle both sides of chicken with salt and pepper. Heat oil in a large nonstick skillet over medium-high heat. Add chicken; cook 5 minutes or until lightly browned. Turn chicken, and cook 6 minutes or until chicken is done. Stir in vinegar, honey, and basil; cook 1 additional minute.
Yield: 4 servings.

Per Serving: Calories 161 (21% from fat)   Fat 3.7g (sat 0.7g)   Protein 26.2g
Carbohydrate 4.6g   Fiber 0.0g   Cholesterol 66mg   Sodium 367mg
Exchanges: 3 Very Lean Meat

•   •   •   •   •

Broccoli Couscous

total time: 10 minutes

Thaw 1 (10-ounce) package frozen chopped broccoli, and drain. Combine 1 (14¼-ounce) can fat-free, reduced-sodium chicken broth, ½ teaspoon salt, and ¼ teaspoon freshly ground pepper in a medium saucepan; bring to a boil. Add 1 cup uncooked couscous and broccoli to broth. Cover, remove from heat, and let stand 5 minutes or until liquid is absorbed. Fluff with a fork.
Yield: 4 servings.

Per Serving: Calories 180 (3% from fat)   Fat 0.6g (sat 0.0g)   Protein 7.8g
Carbohydrate 36.2g   Fiber 3.5g   Cholesterol 0mg   Sodium 399mg
Exchanges: 2 Starch, 1 Vegetable

This glazed chicken is great with or without the basil.

Serve over plain couscous or Broccoli Couscous.

A very tasty and tender chicken.

Serve it to company with Orange Rice, steamed asparagus,

and **Strawberry Shortcakes** (page 220).

TERIYAKI ROAST CHICKEN

work time: 5 minutes • cook time: 1½ hours

1   (3-pound) broiler-fryer
1   small onion, quartered
⅓   cup low-sodium teriyaki sauce
1   teaspoon garlic-pepper seasoning
Cooking spray

Remove giblets from chicken. Reserve for another use. Rinse and drain chicken; pat dry.

Place onion in cavity of chicken. Brush chicken on all sides with some of the teriyaki sauce. Sprinkle with garlic-pepper seasoning. Place chicken, breast side up, on a rack in a roasting pan coated with cooking spray. Insert meat thermometer into meaty part of thigh, making sure it does not touch the bone. Pour remaining teriyaki sauce over chicken.

Bake, uncovered, at 375° for 1½ hours or until meat thermometer registers 185°. Remove skin before serving.

Yield: 6 servings.

Per Serving: Calories 170 (32% from fat)   Fat 6.1g (sat 1.6g)   Protein 24.3g
Carbohydrate 3.0g   Fiber 0.4g   Cholesterol 73mg   Sodium 271mg
Exchanges: 1 Vegetable, 3 Lean Meat

• • • • •

ORANGE RICE

total time: 10 minutes

Prepare 3 cups rice with 2 regular-size bags of boil-in-bag rice cooked according to package directions. Remove rice from bag, and stir in ¼ teaspoon salt, ¼ teaspoon ground ginger, and ½ teaspoon grated orange rind. Garnish with orange slices, if desired.

Yield: 6 (½-cup) servings.

Per Serving: Calories 108 (1% from fat)   Fat 0.1g (sat 0.0g)   Protein 2.0g
Carbohydrate 24.1g   Fiber 0.5g   Cholesterol 0mg   Sodium 98mg
Exchanges: 1½ Starch

Grocery List

1½ pounds fresh
asparagus

1 orange (optional)

1 small onion

Low-sodium teriyaki
sauce

Garlic-pepper seasoning

Ground ginger

Grated orange rind

1 box boil-in-bag rice

1 (3-pound) broiler-fryer

CRANBERRY TURKEY MELTS

total time: 13 minutes

2 **(6-inch) Italian bread shells**
½ cup cranberry-orange sauce
½ pound thinly sliced cooked turkey breast, cut into strips
⅔ cup (2.6 ounces) shredded Pepper-Jack cheese

Place bread shells on ungreased baking sheets. Spread bread shells evenly with cranberry-orange sauce. Arrange turkey strips on top of sauce, and sprinkle with cheese.
Bake at 450° for 8 to 10 minutes or until cheese melts.
Yield: 4 servings.

Per Serving: Calories 345 (26% from fat)   Fat 9.8g (sat 4.7g)   Protein 21.4g
Carbohydrate 38.9g   Fiber 1.1g   Cholesterol 36mg   Sodium 878mg
Exchanges: 2 Starch, 1 Fruit, 2 Medium-Fat Meat

Grocery List

1 stalk celery

1 (16-ounce) package
baby carrots

2 (6-inch) Italian bread
shells (such as Boboli)

1 (12-ounce) container
cranberry-orange sauce

1 (8-ounce) package
shredded Pepper-Jack
cheese

½ pound thinly sliced
cooked turkey breast

Wonderful idea for holiday leftovers or deli-style turkey. Munch on carrot and celery sticks while the pizzalike sandwiches bake.

TURKEY PEPPERONI PIZZA

total time: 13 minutes

Grocery List

1 medium-size sweet red
or green pepper

1 (7.5-ounce) package
fat-free Caesar salad mix

1 (10-ounce) Italian bread
shell (such as Boboli)

1 (14-ounce) jar
pizza sauce

1 package fat-free
oatmeal cookies

1 (6-ounce) package
turkey pepperoni

1 (8-ounce) package
shredded part-skim
mozzarella cheese

1   (10-ounce) Italian bread shell
½   cup pizza sauce
2   ounces turkey pepperoni
1   medium-size sweet red or green pepper, seeded and cut
       into thin slices
1   cup (4 ounces) shredded part-skim mozzarella cheese

Place bread shell on a baking sheet. Spread pizza sauce over shell;
top with pepperoni and pepper slices. Bake at 450° for 10 minutes.
Sprinkle cheese over pizza; bake 2 additional minutes or until
cheese melts. Cut into wedges.
Yield: 6 servings.

Per Serving: Calories 216 (32% from fat)   Fat 7.7g (sat 3.3g)   Protein 14.0g
Carbohydrate 22.3g   Fiber 1.1g   Cholesterol 29mg   Sodium 604mg
Exchanges: 1½ Starch, 1½ Medium-Fat Meat

An easy pizza deserves an easy salad,

so open a bag of fat-free Caesar salad mix.

And while you're opening packages, have some

fat-free oatmeal cookies for dessert.

Start the soup first, then make the quesadillas.

You may like these cheesy quesadillas so much that you skip the soup.

SAUSAGE AND BLACK BEAN SOUP

total time: 16 minutes

Cooking spray
6   ounces turkey kielbasa sausage, sliced
1   cup diced green, sweet red, or yellow pepper
1   (14¼-ounce) can fat-free, reduced-sodium chicken broth
1   (15-ounce) can no-salt-added black beans, rinsed and drained
¼   cup picante sauce or salsa
Chopped cilantro (optional)

Coat a medium saucepan with cooking spray; place over medium-high heat until hot. Add sausage, and sauté 1 minute or until sausage begins to brown. Add pepper; sauté 1 minute.
Add broth; bring to a boil. Reduce heat to low; add beans and picante sauce, and simmer, covered, 5 minutes. Top with cilantro, if desired.
Yield: 4 (1-cup) servings.

Per Serving: Calories 172 (23% from fat)   Fat 4.4g (sat 2.0g)   Protein 12.2g
Carbohydrate 20.5g   Fiber 3.1g   Cholesterol 23mg   Sodium 718mg
Exchanges: 1 Starch, 1 Vegetable, 1 Medium-Fat Meat

• • • • •

SPEEDY QUESADILLAS

total time: 10 minutes

Butter-flavored cooking spray
4   (8-inch) fat-free flour tortillas
1   cup shredded reduced-fat Cheddar cheese
¼   cup chopped green onions

Coat a large nonstick skillet with cooking spray; place over medium-high heat. Place 1 tortilla in skillet, and top with ½ cup cheese, 2 tablespoons onions, and another tortilla. Cook 2 minutes on each side or until lightly browned. Remove from skillet, and keep warm. Repeat with remaining tortillas, cheese, and onions. Cut each quesadilla into 6 wedges.
Yield: 4 servings (serving size: 3 wedges).

Per Serving: Calories 198 (25% from fat)   Fat 5.6g (sat 3.2g)   Protein 11.6g
Carbohydrate 25.0g   Fiber 1.2g   Cholesterol 18mg   Sodium 550mg
Exchanges: 1½ Starch, 1 Medium-Fat Meat

Grocery List

1 medium-size green,
sweet red, or
yellow pepper

1 green onion

Fresh cilantro (optional)

1 (14¼-ounce) can
fat-free, reduced-sodium
chicken broth

1 (15-ounce) can
no-salt-added
black beans

1 (12-ounce) jar
picante sauce or salsa

1 package 8-inch
fat-free flour tortillas

1 (8-ounce) package
shredded reduced-fat
Cheddar cheese

1 (1-pound) package
turkey kielbasa sausage

MEXICALI TURKEY SKILLET CASSEROLE

total time: 14 minutes

4   ounces small elbow macaroni, uncooked
Cooking spray
1   pound freshly ground turkey breast
1   (14½-ounce) can no-salt-added diced tomatoes, undrained
1   (8¾-ounce) can no-salt-added whole-kernel corn, undrained
1   (1.25-ounce) package 40%-less-sodium taco seasoning mix

Cook pasta according to package directions, omitting salt and fat.
While pasta cooks, coat a large nonstick skillet with cooking spray;
place over medium-high heat until hot. Add turkey; cook, stirring
constantly, until turkey crumbles. Stir in drained pasta, tomatoes, corn,
and taco seasoning; cook 5 minutes, stirring occasionally.
Yield: 4 servings.

Per Serving: Calories 330 (8% from fat)   Fat 2.9g (sat 0.6g)   Protein 32.5g
Carbohydrate 42.0g   Fiber 2.7g   Cholesterol 68mg   Sodium 589mg
Exchanges: 2 Starch, 2 Vegetable, 3 Very Lean Meat

• • • • •

GINGERED MELON SALAD

total time: 3 minutes

Combine 4 cups assorted cubed melon (watermelon, cantaloupe,
honeydew). Combine ¼ cup pineapple juice, 1½ tablespoons honey,
and ¼ teaspoon ground ginger; pour over melon cubes, and toss.
Yield: 4 (1-cup) servings.

Per Serving: Calories 89 (4% from fat)   Fat 0.4g (sat 0.2g)   Protein 1.0g
Carbohydrate 22.3g   Fiber 1.3g   Cholesterol 0mg   Sodium 11mg
Exchanges: 1½ Fruit

Kids will love this skillet supper

served with twisted cornbread sticks. Let them pick their

favorite melons to go in the salad.

Grocery List

4 cups assorted cubed melon (watermelon, cantaloupe, honeydew)

1 (6-ounce) can pineapple juice

1 (8¾-ounce) can no-salt-added whole-kernel corn

1 (14½-ounce) can no-salt-added diced tomatoes

Honey

Ground ginger

1 (1.25-ounce) package 40%-less-sodium taco seasoning mix

1 (8-ounce) package small elbow macaroni

1 (9-ounce) can refrigerated cornbread sticks

1 pound freshly ground turkey breast

A hearty warming soup for a cold winter night.
Have a little fun twisting the breadsticks
into pretzel shapes while the soup simmers.

TURKEY-VEGETABLE SOUP

work time: 5 minutes • cook time: 25 minutes

Grocery List

2 (14½-ounce) cans
no-salt-added beef broth

1 (14½-ounce) can
Mexican-style stewed
tomatoes

All-purpose flour

1 (7-ounce) package
refrigerated breadsticks

1 (16-ounce) package
frozen vegetable soup
mix with tomatoes

1 pound freshly ground
raw turkey

Cooking spray
1   pound freshly ground raw turkey
2   (14¼-ounce) cans no-salt-added beef broth, divided
¼   cup all-purpose flour
1   (14½-ounce) can Mexican-style stewed tomatoes, undrained
1   (16-ounce) package frozen vegetable soup mix with tomatoes
¼   teaspoon salt
¼   teaspoon pepper

Coat a Dutch oven with cooking spray; place over medium-high heat until hot. Add turkey; cook, stirring constantly, until it crumbles.
Combine 1 cup broth and flour, stirring until well blended. Add flour mixture, remaining broth, tomatoes, and remaining ingredients to Dutch oven. Bring to a boil; cover, reduce heat to medium, and cook 20 minutes.
Yield: 4 (2-cup) servings.

Per Serving: Calories 295 (13% from fat)   Fat 4.3g (sat 1.2g)   Protein 30.7g
Carbohydrate 29.6g   Fiber 5.0g   Cholesterol 74mg   Sodium 548mg
Exchanges: 2 Starch, 3 Very Lean Meat

• • • • •

PRETZEL BREADSTICKS

total time: 18 minutes

Prepare 1 (7-ounce) package refrigerated breadsticks according to package directions, coating with butter-flavored cooking spray before baking. If desired, shape each breadstick into a pretzel shape before baking.
Yield: 5 breadsticks.

Per Breadstick: Calories 110 (20% from fat)   Fat 2.5g (sat 0.5g)   Protein 3.0g
Carbohydrate 18.0g   Fiber 0.5g   Cholesterol 0mg   Sodium 290mg
Exchanges: 1 Starch, ½ Fat

Grocery List

1 medium-size green
pepper

2 French rolls

1 (26-ounce) jar
tomato-basil pasta sauce

1 (8-ounce) package
angel hair pasta

Olive oil

1 (5.75-ounce) package
classic Italian-seasoned
coating mix for chicken
(such as Shake 'n Bake)

1 (14-ounce) package
fat-free brownies

1 (8-ounce) package
shredded fresh
Parmesan cheese

1 bottle white wine
(optional)

½ pound turkey cutlets

TURKEY PARMESAN

total time: 13 minutes

½ **pound turkey cutlets**
¼ **cup classic Italian-seasoned coating mix for chicken**
Cooking spray
1½ **teaspoons olive oil**
½ **cup tomato-basil pasta sauce**
¼ **cup shredded fresh Parmesan cheese**

Place cutlets between 2 sheets of heavy-duty plastic wrap, and flatten
to ⅛-inch thickness, using a meat mallet or rolling pin. Coat both sides
of cutlets with coating mix.
Coat a nonstick skillet with cooking spray; add olive oil. Place over
medium-high heat until hot. Add cutlets; cook 2 minutes on each side.
Place sauce in a microwave-safe dish; microwave at HIGH 1 minute
or until heated. Spoon over cutlets; sprinkle with cheese.
Yield: 2 servings.

Per Serving: Calories 302 (33% from fat)   Fat 11.1g (sat 3.4g)   Protein 34.1g
Carbohydrate 14.8g   Fiber 1.5g   Cholesterol 78mg   Sodium 894mg
Exchanges: 1 Starch, 4 Lean Meat

• • • • •

SAUTÉED GREEN PEPPER

total time: 7 minutes

Cut 1 medium-size green pepper into strips. Sauté in 1 teaspoon olive
oil in a nonstick skillet until crisp-tender.
Yield: 2 (½-cup) servings.

Per Serving: Calories 29 (74% from fat)   Fat 2.4g (sat 0.3g)   Protein 0.3g
Carbohydrate 2.0g   Fiber 0.6g   Cholesterol 0mg   Sodium 1mg
Exchange: ½ Vegetable

Perfect for a romantic dinner.

Add angel hair pasta, rolls, and fat-free brownies.

And perhaps two glasses of wine?

ORANGE-GLAZED TURKEY WITH CRANBERRY RICE

total time: 9 minutes

Grocery List

1 loaf whole wheat
French bread

1 (14¼-ounce) can
fat-free, reduced-sodium
chicken broth

Low-sugar
orange marmalade

1 (14-ounce) box
instant rice

1 (3-ounce) package
dried cranberries
(such as L'Esprit)

1 (16-ounce) package
frozen green beans

1 pound turkey cutlets

---

1   (14¼-ounce) can fat-free, reduced-sodium chicken broth
1   (3-ounce) package dried cranberries
2   cups instant rice, uncooked
Cooking spray
1   pound turkey cutlets
½   cup low-sugar orange marmalade

Combine broth and cranberries in a medium saucepan; bring to a boil. Stir in rice; remove from heat, cover, and let stand 5 minutes.
Coat a large nonstick skillet with cooking spray; place over medium-high heat until hot. Add turkey, and cook 2 minutes. Turn and cook over high heat 2 minutes or until browned.
Spoon marmalade over turkey; cook, uncovered, over medium heat 2 additional minutes or until thoroughly heated.
Fluff rice mixture with a fork; spoon evenly onto 4 plates, and top each serving with 2 cutlets.
Yield: 4 servings.

Per Serving: Calories 389 (5% from fat)   Fat 2.0g (sat 0.6g)   Protein 30.7g
Carbohydrate 57.8g   Fiber 7.1g   Cholesterol 68mg   Sodium 165mg
Exchanges: 3 Starch, 1 Fruit, 3 Very Lean Meat

A nice and easy departure from
holiday turkey and dressing.

Make it a meal with whole wheat bread
and steamed green beans.

Vegetable Panini with Feta, page 168

On a "Top 10 Lunch and Dinner Entrées" list, six of the ten items are sandwiches.

Sandwiches

Break out of your sandwich slump by using different breads:

- whole wheat buns

- French bread loaves

- flour tortillas

- hoagie rolls

- pita bread rounds

- steak rolls

- kaiser rolls

Check out "Supermarket Bread Basket" on page 10.

Lots of folks think grilled portobellos
taste better than hamburger meat.

PORTOBELLO SANDWICHES

total time: 14 minutes

4   large portobello mushrooms, stems removed
¼   cup fat-free Italian dressing, divided
Cooking spray
4   (1-ounce) slices provolone cheese
4   (2.5-ounce) whole wheat hamburger buns, split
1   (7-ounce) jar roasted red peppers, drained and quartered

Brush both sides of mushrooms evenly with 3 tablespoons Italian dressing. Coat grill rack with cooking spray; place on grill over medium hot coals (350° to 400°). Place mushrooms on rack; grill, covered, 4 minutes on each side or until tender. Place cheese over mushrooms, and grill 1 additional minute to melt cheese.
Brush buns with remaining 1 tablespoon dressing; grill, covered, until lightly toasted. Place mushrooms over bottoms of buns; top with roasted pepper pieces and tops of buns.
Yield: 4 servings.

Per Serving: Calories 287 (31% from fat)   Fat 9.8g (sat 4.9g)   Protein 16.7g
Carbohydrate 39.0g   Fiber 4.9g   Cholesterol 20mg   Sodium 658mg
Exchanges: 2 Starch, 2 Vegetable, 1 High-Fat Meat

Grocery List

4 nectarines

4 large
portobello mushrooms
(about 1¼ pounds)

1 package whole wheat
hamburger buns

1 bottle fat-free
Italian dressing

1 (7-ounce) jar
roasted red peppers

1 (8-ounce) package
sliced provolone cheese

Enjoy these hearty sandwiches with

Greek Pasta Salad (page 218) and fresh nectarines.

2 medium-size ripe
tomatoes

1 medium-size
purple onion

1 (10-ounce) package
romaine salad mix

1 (16-ounce) loaf
French bread
(about 20 inches long)

1 (16-ounce) can
no-salt-added
kidney beans

4 (10¾-ounce) cans
low-sodium tomato soup

1 bottle fat-free
Caesar dressing

Lemon juice

1 (2.8-ounce) container
pesto

1 (8-ounce) carton plain
low-fat yogurt

1 (4-ounce) package
crumbled feta cheese

VEGETABLE PANINI WITH FETA

total time: 10 minutes

1   (16-ounce) loaf French bread (about 20 inches long)
1   (10-ounce) package romaine salad mix
1   (16-ounce) can no-salt-added kidney beans, rinsed and drained
2   medium-size ripe tomatoes, coarsely chopped
½   medium-size purple onion, thinly sliced
½   cup (2 ounces) crumbled feta cheese
⅓   cup fat-free Caesar dressing
2   tablespoons lemon juice

Cut a ½-inch-thick slice from top of bread, and set top aside. Hollow out bread using a serrated knife, leaving a 1-inch shell; reserve soft bread for another use. Set bread shell aside.
Combine salad mix and next 4 ingredients. Combine dressing and lemon juice; drizzle over lettuce mixture. Toss.
Fill bread shell with lettuce mixture; replace top. Slice and serve.
Yield: 8 servings.

Per Serving: Calories 264 (10% from fat)   Fat 3.0g (sat 1.5g)   Protein 10.5g
Carbohydrate 47.9g   Fiber 4.2g   Cholesterol 8mg   Sodium 602mg
Exchanges: 3 Starch, 1 Vegetable, ½ Fat

• • • • •

TOMATO SOUP WITH PESTO

total time: 9 minutes

4   (10¾-ounce) cans low-sodium tomato soup
3   cups water
½   cup plain low-fat yogurt
2   tablespoons pesto

Combine 4 (10¾-ounce) cans low-sodium tomato soup and 3 cups water in a saucepan; cook over medium heat until thoroughly heated. Combine yogurt and pesto, stirring well. Drizzle 1 tablespoon pesto mixture over each serving.
Yield: 8 (1-cup) servings.

Per Serving: Calories 132 (20% from fat)   Fat 3.0g (sat 1.0g)   Protein 2.3g
Carbohydrate 23.8g   Fiber 1.3g   Cholesterol 1mg   Sodium 608mg
Exchanges: 1½ Starch, ½ Fat

A sandwich packed full of veggies and cheese,
and a tasty soup that starts from cans.

Grocery List

4 tangerines

1 medium-size tomato

1 small onion

1 large green pepper

1 (12-ounce) jar salsa (optional)

1 (12-ounce) jar fat-free black bean dip (such as Guiltless Gourmet)

1 package 10-inch fat-free flour tortillas

1 (8-ounce) carton fat-free sour cream (optional)

BLACK BEAN BURRITOS

total time: 15 minutes

1   (12-ounce) jar fat-free black bean dip
4   (10-inch) fat-free flour tortillas
1   cup chopped tomato
¾   cup chopped onion
1   cup chopped green pepper
Salsa (optional)
Fat-free sour cream (optional)

Spread dip evenly over tortillas (about ⅓ cup dip per tortilla). Sprinkle evenly with tomato, onion, and green pepper.
To serve, roll up tortillas. If desired, top with salsa and sour cream.
Yield: 4 servings.

Per Serving: Calories 225 (1% from fat)   Fat 0.3g (sat 0.0g)   Protein 9.9g
Carbohydrate 44.4g   Fiber 5.4g   Cholesterol 0mg   Sodium 645mg
Exchanges: 2 Starch, 2 Vegetable

A super-easy, no-cook sandwich.

Serve with **Marinated Cucumbers and Tomatoes** (page 215)

and juicy tangerines.

Grocery List

1 large sweet red pepper

1 large green pepper

1 large onion

1 package steak rolls

1 jar unsweetened applesauce

Dried oregano (optional)

Cinnamon-sugar

2 (8-ounce) cartons vanilla low-fat yogurt

½ pound lean roast beef

HOT BEEF AND PEPPER ROLLS

total time: 17 minutes

Olive oil-flavored cooking spray
½ **pound thinly sliced lean roast beef, cut into strips**
1 **large sweet red pepper, seeded and thinly sliced**
1 **large green pepper, seeded and thinly sliced**
1 **large onion, thinly sliced**
4 **(2.8-ounce) steak rolls, split and warmed**
½ **teaspoon dried oregano (optional)**

Coat a large nonstick skillet with cooking spray; place over medium-high heat until hot. Add meat, peppers, and onion; sauté until meat is hot and onion is tender. Spoon meat mixture evenly onto bottom halves of rolls. Sprinkle with oregano, if desired, and top with remaining roll halves.
Yield: 4 servings.

Per Serving: Calories 373 (19% from fat)   Fat 8.0g (sat 2.3g)   Protein 21.8g
Carbohydrate 56.1g   Fiber 5.0g   Cholesterol 66mg   Sodium 821mg
Exchanges: 3 Starch, 2 Vegetable, 1 Lean Meat, 1 Fat

•　•　•　•　•

CINNAMON-APPLE YOGURT

total time: 2 minutes

Spoon ½ cup vanilla low-fat yogurt into each of 4 dessert dishes. Top each with 2 tablespoons unsweetened applesauce and 1 teaspoon cinnamon-sugar.
Yield: 4 servings.

Per Serving: Calories 114 (12% from fat)   Fat 1.5g (sat 0.9g)   Protein 5.7g
Carbohydrate 20.4g   Fiber 0.5g   Cholesterol 6mg   Sodium 76mg
Exchanges: 1 Starch, ½ Skim Milk

A great way to make a meal

from leftover roast beef or beef from the deli.

An easy dessert is Cinnamon-Apple Yogurt.

Grocery List

1 package hoagie rolls

1 jar creamy mustard blend
(such as Dijonnaise)

1 (8-ounce) package shredded part-skim mozzarella cheese

1 (16-ounce) package frozen pepper stir-fry

1 (9-ounce) package frozen seasoned beef strips

PHILLY CHEESESTEAK SANDWICHES

total time: 21 minutes

1 (16-ounce) package frozen pepper stir-fry
1 (9-ounce) package frozen seasoned beef strips
2 tablespoons creamy mustard blend
6 (2.5-ounce) hoagie rolls
¾ cup (3 ounces) shredded part-skim mozzarella cheese

Heat a large nonstick skillet over medium-high heat until hot; add frozen pepper stir-fry, and cook 2 minutes. Add beef strips, and cook 3 to 5 minutes or until thoroughly heated; drain.

Spread 1 teaspoon mustard blend on bottom half of each roll. Spoon ½ cup beef mixture onto each roll; top with cheese and top half of roll. Wrap each sandwich in aluminum foil. Bake at 350° for 6 to 7 minutes or until cheese melts. Remove sandwiches from foil; serve immediately.

Yield: 6 servings.

Per Serving: Calories 310 (24% from fat)   Fat 8.1g (sat 3.5g)   Protein 21.1g
Carbohydrate 41.9g   Fiber 3.2g   Cholesterol 36mg   Sodium 688mg
Exchanges: 2 Starch, 2 Vegetable, 2 Medium-Fat Meat

A meal on a roll.

For dessert, try the **Strawberry Sundaes** on page 221.

SAUCY DOGS

total time: 12 minutes

Grocery List

1 medium onion

1 (16-ounce) package
coleslaw mix

1 package hot dog buns

1 (15-ounce) can
sloppy joe sauce

Celery seeds

1 bottle fat-free
honey-mustard dressing

1 (1-pound) package
low-fat frankfurters

½ pound ground round

½   **pound ground round**
1   **cup chopped onion**
1   **(15-ounce) can sloppy joe sauce**
8   **low-fat frankfurters**
8   **hot dog buns**

Combine beef and onion in a medium nonstick skillet over medium-high heat. Cook until beef is browned and onion is tender, stirring until meat crumbles. Drain, if necessary, and return to skillet.

Add sloppy joe sauce to beef mixture, and bring to a boil. Reduce heat, and simmer 5 minutes, stirring occasionally.

While sauce cooks, cook frankfurters according to package directions. Place 1 frankfurter in each bun. Spoon beef mixture evenly over frankfurters.

Yield: 8 servings.

Per Serving: Calories 278 (21% from fat)   Fat 6.6g (sat 1.7g)   Protein 15.4g
Carbohydrate 36.2g   Fiber 0.9g   Cholesterol 47mg   Sodium 806mg
Exchanges: 2 Starch, 1 Vegetable, 1 Medium-Fat Meat

•   •   •   •   •

HONEY-KISSED SLAW

total time: 5 minutes

Combine 4 cups coleslaw mix, ½ teaspoon celery seeds, ½ teaspoon pepper, and ½ cup fat-free honey-mustard dressing; toss gently.
Yield: 8 (½-cup) servings.

Per Serving: Calories 34 (3% from fat)   Fat 0.1g (sat 0.0g)   Protein 0.5g
Carbohydrate 8.0g   Fiber 0.9g   Cholesterol 0mg   Sodium 152mg
Exchange: 1 Vegetable

Better than the dogs at the downtown hot dog stand.

Serve them with napkins and Honey-Kissed Slaw.

Let the beans simmer while you grill the burgers.

CHILI BACON BURGERS

total time: 15 minutes

1   (1-pound) package ground sirloin patties (4 patties)
2   teaspoons salt-free cowboy barbecue rub
¼   cup nonfat mayonnaise
¼   cup chunky salsa
2   tablespoons bacon bits
4   lettuce leaves
4   (2-ounce) hamburger buns with sesame seeds
4   thin slices sweet onion
4   slices tomato

Rub both sides of sirloin patties with barbecue rub. Place patties on grill over medium-hot coals (350° to 400°); grill, covered, 6 minutes on each side or until done.
While meat cooks, combine mayonnaise, salsa, and bacon bits.
Place lettuce leaves on bottom halves of buns; place patties on lettuce. Top with onion, tomato, 2 tablespoons mayonnaise mixture, and remaining bun halves.
Yield: 4 servings.

Per Serving: Calories 402 (27% from fat)   Fat 12.0g (sat 3.4g)   Protein 32.8g
Carbohydrate 38.9g   Fiber 1.4g   Cholesterol 100mg   Sodium 541mg
Exchanges: 2½ Starch, 4 Lean Meat

• • • • •

BAKED BEANS IN A POT

total time: 15 minutes

Drain 1 (15-ounce) can no-salt-added kidney or pinto beans. Combine drained beans, 3 tablespoons brown sugar, 2 tablespoons dried onion flakes, and ¼ cup barbecue sauce in a medium saucepan. Bring to a boil; cover, reduce heat, and simmer 5 minutes. Uncover, and cook 5 additional minutes.
Yield: 4 servings.

Per Serving: Calories 128 (4% from fat)   Fat 0.6g (sat 0.1g)   Protein 6.3g
Carbohydrate 25.1g   Fiber 2.6g   Cholesterol 0mg   Sodium 148mg
Exchanges: 1½ Starch

Grocery List

1 small head lettuce

1 small sweet onion

1 large tomato

1 package hamburger buns with sesame seeds

1 (15-ounce) can no-salt-added kidney or pinto beans

Barbecue sauce

1 (12-ounce) jar chunky salsa

Nonfat mayonnaise

1 jar bacon bits (such as Hormel)

Salt-free cowboy barbecue rub (such as Spice Hunter)

Dried onion flakes

Brown sugar

1 (1-pound) package ground sirloin patties (4 patties)

HORSERADISH HAMBURGERS

total time: 17 minutes

1 **pound ground sirloin**
¼ **cup Italian-seasoned breadcrumbs**
1½ **tablespoons prepared horseradish**
Cooking spray
4 **(½-inch-thick) slices purple onion**
4 **(2.25-ounce) kaiser rolls, split and toasted**
Mustard (optional)
Ketchup (optional)

Combine first 3 ingredients, stirring well; shape into 4 (½-inch-thick) patties.

Coat grill rack with cooking spray; place on grill over medium-hot coals (350° to 400°). Place meat patties and onion slices on rack; grill, covered, 5 minutes on each side or until meat is done. Place 1 pattie and 1 onion slice on bottom half of each roll. If desired, add mustard and ketchup. Top with remaining roll half.

Yield: 4 servings.

Note: To broil, coat broiler pan with cooking spray; place meat patties and onion slices on broiler pan. Broil, 3 inches from heat, 5 minutes on each side or until done.

Per Serving: Calories 418 (22% from fat)   Fat 10.4g (sat 2.5g)   Protein 34.2g
Carbohydrate 45.4g   Fiber 1.4g   Cholesterol 76mg   Sodium 681mg
Exchanges: 3 Starch, 4 Lean Meat

Grill or broil these high-flavor hamburgers.
Open a bag of low-fat potato chips and a container of

low-fat coleslaw from the deli.

"Bueno" means "good" in Spanish,

and these burritos are. They're even better with

Mexican Corn Salad.

BUENOS BURRITOS

total time: 15 minutes

Cooking spray
½ pound chicken breast tenders
1 cup diced sweet red pepper
½ cup salsa, divided
1 cup canned fat-free refried beans
4 (8-inch) fat-free flour tortillas

Coat a large nonstick skillet with cooking spray; place over medium-high heat until hot. Add chicken and pepper; sauté 3 minutes. Add ¼ cup salsa; reduce heat to medium-low, and cook, 2 minutes, stirring occasionally.

While chicken cooks, combine refried beans and remaining ¼ cup salsa in a small microwave-safe bowl. Cover with heavy-duty plastic wrap, and vent. Microwave at HIGH 2 minutes or until thoroughly heated, stirring after 1 minute.

Wrap tortillas in heavy-duty plastic wrap. Microwave at HIGH 30 to 45 seconds or until warm. Spread bean mixture evenly down centers of tortillas; top evenly with chicken mixture. Roll up tortillas.

Yield: 4 servings.

Per Serving: Calories 242 (4% from fat)   Fat 1.1g (sat 0.2g)   Protein 19.8g
Carbohydrate 37.0g   Fiber 5.1g   Cholesterol 33mg   Sodium 759mg
Exchanges: 2 Starch, 1 Vegetable, 2 Very Lean Meat

• • • • •

MEXICAN CORN SALAD

total time: 5 minutes

Combine 2 cups frozen corn, thawed, ½ cup salsa, 1 green onion, sliced, and 3 tablespoons chopped radish. Spoon mixture evenly over 4 large romaine lettuce leaves.

Yield: 4 servings.

Per Serving: Calories 80 (6% from fat)   Fat 0.5g (sat 0.1g)   Protein 3.0g
Carbohydrate 19.1g   Fiber 2.8g   Cholesterol 0mg   Sodium 149mg
Exchange: 1 Starch

Grocery List

1 head romaine lettuce

1 (6-ounce) package
radishes

1 green onion

1 sweet red pepper

1 (16-ounce) can
fat-free refried beans

1 (12-ounce) jar salsa

1 package 8-inch
fat-free flour tortillas

1 (10-ounce) package
frozen corn

½ pound chicken breast
tenders

Enjoy these Mexican-style wrapped sandwiches with Green Chile Refried Beans and fat-free salsa-flavored tortilla chips.

TACO CHICKEN TORTILLA WRAPS

total time: 15 minutes

4   (8-inch) fat-free flour tortillas
1   pound chicken breast tenders
1   (1.25-ounce) package 40%-less-sodium taco seasoning mix
Cooking spray
1   cup thin onion wedges
2   cups shredded iceberg lettuce
1   medium-size tomato, chopped
½   cup fat-free sour cream

Wrap tortillas in aluminum foil; bake at 375° for 10 minutes or until thoroughly heated.

While tortillas bake, combine chicken and taco seasoning in a heavy-duty, zip-top plastic bag. Seal bag; shake well.

Coat a large nonstick skillet with cooking spray; place over medium-high heat until hot. Add chicken and onion; sauté 6 minutes or until chicken is done.

Spoon chicken mixture evenly onto tortillas; top evenly with lettuce, tomato, and sour cream. Roll up tortillas, and wrap in unbleached parchment paper, if desired. Serve immediately.

Yield: 4 servings.

Per Serving: Calories 299 (5% from fat)   Fat 1.8g (sat 0.4g)   Protein 32.0g
Carbohydrate 36.3g   Fiber 2.1g   Cholesterol 66mg   Sodium 770mg
Exchanges: 2 Starch, 1 Vegetable, 3 Very Lean Meat

• • • • •

GREEN CHILE REFRIED BEANS

total time: 5 minutes

Combine 1 (15-ounce) can fat-free refried beans with green chiles and 2 tablespoons salsa in a small saucepan. Cook over medium heat just until heated, stirring often.

Yield: 4 servings.

Per Serving: Calories 98 (0% from fat)   Fat 0.0g (sat 0.0g)   Protein 6.2g
Carbohydrate 17.9g   Fiber 4.5g   Cholesterol 0mg   Sodium 441mg
Exchange: 1 Starch

ORIENTAL CHICKEN WRAPS

total time: 14 minutes

1   teaspoon vegetable oil
2   cups broccoli slaw
1   cup sliced fresh mushrooms
1   (9-ounce) package frozen cooked diced chicken
⅓   cup fat-free, reduced-sodium chicken broth
½   teaspoon garlic-pepper seasoning
1   tablespoon low-sodium soy sauce
1½ teaspoons cornstarch
4   (6-inch) flour tortillas

Heat oil in a large nonstick skillet over medium-high heat. Add broccoli slaw and mushrooms; cook 3 to 4 minutes or until crisp-tender, stirring occasionally.

Add chicken, broth, and garlic-pepper to skillet; stir. Cover and cook over medium heat 3 minutes or until thoroughly heated. Combine soy sauce and cornstarch, stirring until smooth. Add to skillet; cook, stirring constantly, 1 minute or until slightly thickened. Spoon one-fourth chicken mixture down center of each tortilla. Roll up tortillas; serve immediately.

Yield: 4 servings.

Per Serving: Calories 256 (22% from fat)   Fat 6.2g (sat 1.3g)   Protein 24.9g
Carbohydrate 23.8g   Fiber 2.8g   Cholesterol 54mg   Sodium 451mg
Exchanges: 1 Starch, 2 Vegetable, 2 Lean Meat

• • • • •

BOK CHOY AND TOMATO SALAD

total time: 8 minutes

Combine 4 cups sliced bok choy or napa cabbage, 3 plum tomatoes, chopped, and 1 small yellow squash, chopped. Drizzle with ¼ cup fat-free toasted sesame soy and ginger vinaigrette; toss.

Yield: 4 (1¼-cup) servings.

Per Serving: Calories 51 (5% from fat)   Fat 0.3g (sat 0.0g)   Protein 1.5g
Carbohydrate 11.3g   Fiber 2.5g   Cholesterol 0mg   Sodium 112mg
Exchanges: 2 Vegetable

Sort of like an egg roll, but wrapped in a tortilla.

Keep the Asian theme with Bok Choy and Tomato Salad.

This is one tasty sandwich!
Both the pita and Balsamic Tomato Salad are
packed with wonderful high-flavor ingredients
for a very satisfying meal.

GREEK CHICKEN PITAS

total time: 12 minutes

Cooking spray
1   **pound chicken breast tenders**
1   **teaspoon Greek seasoning**
½   **cup hummus**
4   **(8-inch) pita bread rounds**
1   **cup torn romaine lettuce**
2   **plum tomatoes, sliced**
1   **small cucumber, cut into strips**
¼   **cup (2 ounces) crumbled basil- and tomato-flavored feta cheese**

Coat a large nonstick skillet with cooking spray; place over medium-high heat until hot. Sprinkle chicken with Greek seasoning; add to skillet. Cook chicken 6 to 8 minutes or until lightly browned, stirring occasionally.

While chicken cooks, spread hummus evenly over pita rounds. Arrange chicken, lettuce, and remaining ingredients evenly on one half of each pita round. Fold pitas over filling; secure with wooden picks.

Yield: 4 servings.

Per Serving: Calories 314 (15% from fat)   Fat 5.3g (sat 2.6g)   Protein 33.4g
Carbohydrate 30.9g   Fiber 1.8g   Cholesterol 78mg   Sodium 751mg
Exchanges: 2 Starch, 4 Very Lean Meat

• • • • •

BALSAMIC TOMATO SALAD

total time: 5 minutes

Combine 4 plum tomatoes, 2 green onions, chopped, and ¼ cup fat-free balsamic vinaigrette. Sprinkle with cracked black pepper, if desired. **Yield:** 4 servings.

Per Serving: Calories 28 (6% from fat)   Fat 0.2g (sat 0.0g)   Protein 0.7g
Carbohydrate 6.5g   Fiber 1.0g   Cholesterol 0mg   Sodium 207mg
Exchange: 1 Vegetable

Grocery List

1 head romaine lettuce

6 plum tomatoes

1 small cucumber

2 green onions

1 package pita bread rounds

1 (8-ounce) container hummus

Greek seasoning

1 bottle fat-free balsamic vinaigrette

1 (4-ounce) package crumbled basil- and tomato-flavored feta cheese

1 pound chicken breast tenders

total time: 13 minutes

¾   **pound freshly ground raw turkey breast**
1   **medium onion, chopped**
1   **(8-ounce) can no-salt-added tomato sauce**
1   **(7-ounce) jar roasted red peppers, drained and chopped**
¼   **teaspoon salt**
¼   **teaspoon pepper**
2   **teaspoons liquid mesquite smoke (optional)**
4   **(2.25-ounce) whole wheat or plain kaiser rolls**

Cook turkey and chopped onion in a nonstick skillet over medium-high heat 4 to 5 minutes or until onion is tender and turkey is done, stirring until turkey crumbles. Stir in tomato sauce and red peppers; simmer 5 minutes.
Stir in salt, pepper, and, if desired, liquid smoke. Spoon turkey mixture evenly onto bottom halves of rolls, and top with remaining roll halves.
Yield: 4 servings.

Per Serving: Calories 346 (14% from fat)   Fat 5.2g (sat 0.5g)   Protein 28.1g
Carbohydrate 45.6g   Fiber 1.9g   Cholesterol 51mg   Sodium 665mg
Exchanges: 3 Starch, 3 Very Lean Meat

·   ·   ·   ·   ·

VEGETABLE CRUDITÉS

total time: 5 minutes

Arrange ¼ pound baby carrots, 1 cucumber, sliced, and ¼ pound each of cauliflower and broccoli flowerets on a large platter. Serve with ½ cup fat-free Ranch-style dressing.
Yield: 4 servings.

Per Serving: Calories 85 (3% from fat)   Fat 0.3g (sat 0.1g)   Protein 3.0g
Carbohydrate 18.7g   Fiber 2.8g   Cholesterol 0mg   Sodium 339mg
Exchanges: 2 Vegetable, ½ Starch

Grocery List

2 cups low-fat
deli potato salad

1 medium onion

1 (8-ounce) package
baby carrots

1 cucumber

¼ pound fresh
cauliflower flowerets

¼ pound fresh
broccoli flowerets

1 package whole wheat
or plain kaiser rolls

1 (8-ounce) can no-salt-
added tomato sauce

1 bottle fat-free
Ranch-style dressing

1 (7-ounce) jar
roasted red peppers

Liquid mesquite smoke
(optional)

¾ pound freshly ground
raw turkey breast

Celebrate the 4th of July by being free from kitchen duty. Enjoy **BBQ sandwiches,** low-fat deli potato salad, and fresh veggies.

Chili Grande, page 197

67% of households with children eat a
meal together at least five days a week.

Slow Cooker Suppers

What's fast about a slow cooker?

- 5 ingredients (or less)

- 5 minutes of work time

- 4 to 8 hours of free time
  while your supper cooks

Grocery List

2 medium zucchini

1 sun-dried tomato
bread round

2 (14.5-ounce) cans
Italian-style diced
tomatoes

Cinnamon sticks or
ground cinnamon

¾ pound beef stew meat

MEDITERRANEAN BEEF STEW

work time: 5 minutes • cook time: 5 hours or 8 hours

2   medium zucchini, cut into bite-size chunks
¾   pound beef stew meat, cut into ½-inch pieces
2   (14.5-ounce) cans Italian-style diced tomatoes, undrained
½   teaspoon pepper
1   (2-inch) stick cinnamon or ¼ teaspoon ground cinnamon

Place zucchini in bottom of a 3½-quart electric slow cooker. Add beef and remaining ingredients. Cover and cook on high setting 5 hours or until meat is tender. Or, cover and cook on high setting 1 hour; reduce to low setting, and cook 7 hours. Remove and discard cinnamon stick before serving.
Yield: 4 servings.

Per Serving: Calories 193 (19% from fat)   Fat 4.0g (sat 1.3g)   Protein 22.8g
Carbohydrate 16.9g   Fiber 1.5g   Cholesterol 48mg   Sodium 572mg
Exchanges: 1 Starch, 3 Very Lean Meat

The day can't go by fast enough when this hearty stew is waiting for you. Pick up some sun-dried tomato bread at the grocery deli or bakery on your way home.

Grand chili! The longer it simmers, the better the flavor.
The bowls taste good, too.

CHILI GRANDE

work time: 5 minutes • cook time: 4 hours or 8 hours

¾ **pound beef stew meat, cut into ½-inch pieces**
1 **tablespoon salt-free Mexican seasoning**
2 **(15½-ounce) cans chili beans in zesty sauce, undrained**
1 **(14½-ounce) can no-salt-added stewed tomatoes, undrained**
1 **(10-ounce) package frozen chopped green pepper (about 3 cups)**
1 **cup chopped frozen onion**
Fat-free sour cream (optional)
Chopped fresh cilantro (optional)

Place first 6 ingredients in a 4- or 5-quart electric slow cooker; stir well.
Cover and cook on high setting 4 hours. Or, cover and cook on high setting 1 hour; reduce to low setting, and cook 7 hours.
If desired, spoon chili into Tortilla Bowls, and top with sour cream and cilantro (bowls not included in analysis).
Yield: 6 (1½-cup) servings.

Per Serving: Calories 256 (14% from fat) Fat 4.0g (sat 0.9g) Protein 22.9g
Carbohydrate 38.3g Fiber 9.4g Cholesterol 32mg Sodium 722mg
Exchanges: 2 Starch, 2 Vegetable, 2 Lean Meat

• • • • •

TORTILLA BOWLS

total time: 12 minutes (about 2 minutes per bowl)

For each bowl, line a 1½-quart glass bowl with 1 (10-inch) flour tortilla. Prick holes in the bottom of tortilla with a fork. Microwave at HIGH 2 to 3 minutes or until crisp. Remove from oven, and let cool slightly in glass bowl. Remove tortilla from bowl. Place tortilla bowl in a shallow dish; spoon chili into tortilla bowl.
Yield: 6 bowls.

Per Bowl: Calories 161 (20% from fat) Fat 3.5g (sat 0.6g) Protein 4.3g
Carbohydrate 27.6g Fiber 1.5g Cholesterol 0mg Sodium 237mg
Exchanges: 2 Starch

Grocery List

Fresh cilantro (optional)

2 (15½-ounce) cans chili beans in zesty sauce

1 (14½-ounce) can no-salt-added stewed tomatoes

Salt-free Mexican seasoning

1 package 10-inch flour tortillas

Fat-free sour cream (optional)

1 (10-ounce) package frozen chopped onion

1 (10-ounce) package frozen chopped green pepper

¾ pound beef stew meat

ITALIAN POT ROAST

work time: 5 minutes • cook time: 5 hours or 8 hours

Grocery List

2 (10-ounce) packages
Italian-style salad greens

1 medium onion

8 French rolls

2 (8-ounce) cans
no-salt-added
tomato sauce

1 (0.7-ounce) package
Italian salad
dressing mix

1 (7-ounce) jar roasted
red pepper strips

1 bottle fat-free
Italian dressing

1 (2½-pound) boneless
beef round roast

1   (2½-pound) boneless beef round roast
1   medium onion, sliced
¼   teaspoon salt
¼   teaspoon pepper
2   (8-ounce) cans no-salt-added tomato sauce
1   (0.7-ounce) package Italian salad dressing mix

Slice roast in half for even cooking; place in a 3½-quart electric slow cooker. Add onion and remaining ingredients. Cover and cook on high setting 5 hours or until roast is tender. Or, cover and cook on high setting 1 hour; reduce to low setting, and cook 7 hours. Slice meat to serve.
Yield: 8 servings.

Per Serving: Calories 223 (23% from fat)   Fat 5.8g (sat 2.1g)   Protein 33.3g
Carbohydrate 7.4g   Fiber 1.2g   Cholesterol 81mg   Sodium 473mg
Exchanges: 1 Vegetable, 4 Very Lean Meat

• • • • •

ITALIAN-STYLE SALAD

total time: 3 minutes

Combine 2 (10-ounce) packages Italian-style salad greens and 1 (7-ounce) jar roasted red pepper strips, drained. Drizzle with ⅔ cup fat-free Italian dressing.
Yield: 8 (½-cup) servings.

Per Serving: Calories 28 (6% from fat)   Fat 0.2g (sat 0.0g)   Protein 1.5g
Carbohydrate 5.6g   Fiber 1.2g   Cholesterol 0mg   Sodium 237mg
Exchange: 1 Vegetable

Better than the average pot roast—the Italian flavor makes it special. Serve with Italian-Style Salad and hot rolls.

BARBECUE PORK CHOPS

work time: 10 minutes   •   cook time: 4 hours or 8 hours

Grocery List

1 (16-ounce) package
broccoli slaw

1 medium-size
Red Delicious apple

1 green onion

1 (14½-ounce) can
no-salt-added
stewed tomatoes

Apple juice

Cider vinegar

Sugar

Thick-and-spicy honey
barbecue sauce

1 box boil-in-bag rice

1 (10-ounce) package
frozen vegetable
seasoning blend

8 (5-ounce) center-cut
pork chops

8   (5-ounce) center-cut pork chops (½ inch thick)
¼   teaspoon pepper
Cooking spray
½   cup thick-and-spicy honey barbecue sauce
1   (14½-ounce) can no-salt-added stewed tomatoes, undrained
1   (10-ounce) package frozen vegetable seasoning blend

Trim fat from chops; sprinkle chops with pepper. Coat a large nonstick skillet with cooking spray; place over medium-high heat until hot. Add chops, in two batches, and cook until browned on both sides. Coat a 3½- or 4-quart electric slow cooker with cooking spray. Place chops in cooker.
Combine barbecue sauce, tomatoes, and frozen vegetable blend, stirring well; pour mixture over chops. Cover and cook on high setting 4 hours. Or, cover and cook on high setting 1 hour; reduce to low setting, and cook 7 hours.
Yield: 8 servings.

Per Serving: Calories 237 (31% from fat)   Fat 8.2g (sat 2.8g)   Protein 25.9g
Carbohydrate 12.4g   Fiber 0.8g   Cholesterol 72mg   Sodium 250mg
Exchanges: 2 Vegetable, 3 Lean Meat

• • • • •

QUICK VEGGIE SLAW

total time: 7 minutes

Combine 1 (16-ounce) package broccoli slaw, 1 Red Delicious apple, chopped, and 1 green onion, chopped, in a large bowl. Combine ½ cup cider vinegar, ¼ cup apple juice, ⅓ cup sugar, ¼ teaspoon salt, and ¼ teaspoon pepper, stirring well. Pour vinegar mixture over slaw mixture, and toss. Serve immediately, or cover and chill.
Yield: 9 (1-cup) servings.

Per Serving: Calories 60 (2% from fat)   Fat 0.1g (sat 0.0g)   Protein 0.7g
Carbohydrate 14.7g   Fiber 1.4g   Cholesterol 0mg   Sodium 74mg
Exchange: 1 Fruit

These saucy chops are great served over rice. Make Quick Veggie Slaw the night before so supper's ready when the chops are.

Make your meal really Moroccan

with couscous and Toasted Pita Chips.

MOROCCAN CHICKEN AND LENTILS

work time: 2 minutes • cook time: 5 hours or 8 hours

1	(8-ounce) package baby carrots
1½	cups lentils, uncooked
1½	pounds frozen chicken breast tenders
2	tablespoons minced garlic
¾	teaspoon salt
2	teaspoons salt-free Moroccan rub (or ¾ teaspoon ground turmeric, ½ teaspoon ground red pepper, and ½ teaspoon ground cinnamon)
2	(14¼-ounce) cans fat-free, reduced-sodium chicken broth

Place all ingredients, in order listed, in a 4- or 5-quart electric slow cooker. Cover and cook on high setting 5 hours. Or, cover and cook on high setting 1 hour; reduce to low setting, and cook 7 hours.
Yield: 6 (1-cup) servings.

Per Serving: Calories 320 (5% from fat)   Fat 2.0g (sat 0.5g)   Protein 40.5g
Carbohydrate 33.3g   Fiber 6.7g   Cholesterol 66mg   Sodium 388mg
Exchanges: 2 Starch, 1 Vegetable, 4 Very Lean Meat

• • • • •

TOASTED PITA CHIPS

total time: 10 minutes

Split 3 pita bread rounds in half horizontally. Cut each half into 8 wedges. Arrange wedges, rough side up, on a baking sheet, and generously spray with butter-flavored cooking spray. Bake at 400° for 6 to 7 minutes or until crisp and golden.
Yield: 6 servings (serving size: 8 wedges).

Per Serving: Calories 77 (11% from fat)   Fat 0.9g (sat 0.0g)   Protein 1.4g
Carbohydrate 14.1g   Fiber 2.6g   Cholesterol 0mg   Sodium 349mg
Exchange: 1 Starch

Grocery List

1 (8-ounce) package baby carrots

1 package pita bread rounds

2 (14¼-ounce) cans fat-free, reduced-sodium chicken broth

1 (4½-ounce) jar minced garlic

Salt-free Moroccan rub (such as Spice Hunter) or ground turmeric, ground red pepper, and ground cinnamon

1 (10-ounce) box couscous

1 (16-ounce) package lentils

1½ pounds frozen chicken breast tenders

Fruited Chicken and Barley

work time: 5 minutes • cook time: 4 hours or 8 hours

1¼ cups pearl barley, uncooked
6 cups water
2 pounds skinned chicken thighs
1 large onion, coarsely chopped
1 (8-ounce) package dried mixed fruit
1 tablespoon salt-free Caribbean spice rub
½ teaspoon salt
¼ teaspoon pepper

Combine all ingredients in a 4-quart electric slow cooker; stir well. Cover and cook on high setting 4 hours or until chicken is tender. Or, cover and cook on high setting 1 hour; reduce to low setting, and cook 7 hours.
Yield: 6 (2-cup) servings.

Per Serving: Calories 399 (12% from fat) Fat 5.2g (sat 1.3g) Protein 28.8g
Carbohydrate 58.3g Fiber 9.7g Cholesterol 99mg Sodium 316mg
Exchanges: 3 Starch, 1 Fruit, 3 Very Lean Meat

Grocery List

1 large onion

6 multigrain rolls

Salt-free
Caribbean spice rub

1 (8-ounce) package
dried mixed fruit

1 (16-ounce) package
pearl barley

2 pounds skinned
chicken thighs

What you need after a long, hard day

is this "stick-to-your-ribs" chicken dinner.

Round out your meal with multigrain rolls.

Grocery List

2 large bananas

1 loaf French bread

1 (14½-ounce) can
Cajun-style stewed
tomatoes

1 (14¼-ounce) can
fat-free, reduced-sodium
chicken broth

Salt-free extra-spicy
seasoning

Brown sugar

1 jar fat-free
caramel topping

1 box boil-in-bag rice

1 (14-ounce) package
low-fat smoked sausage
(such as Healthy Choice)

1 (16-ounce) package
frozen vegetable
gumbo mixture

½ gallon vanilla fat-free
ice cream

1 pound skinned, boned
chicken breast halves

HEARTY CHICKEN-SAUSAGE SOUP

work time: 7 minutes • cook time: 4 hours or 8 hours

1 (16-ounce) package frozen vegetable gumbo mixture
1 pound skinned, boned chicken breast halves, cut into 1-inch
     pieces
4 ounces low-fat smoked sausage, sliced
1 (14½-ounce) can Cajun-style stewed tomatoes, undrained
1 (14¼-ounce) can fat-free, reduced-sodium chicken broth
2 teaspoons salt-free extra-spicy seasoning
2 cups cooked long-grain rice, cooked without salt or fat

Place first 6 ingredients in a 3½-quart electric slow cooker. Cover and cook on high setting 4 hours. Or, cover and cook on high setting 1 hour; reduce to low setting, and cook 7 hours. Stir in cooked rice during last 30 minutes of cooking time.
Yield: 6 (1¼-cup) servings.

Per Serving: Calories 240 (6% from fat)   Fat 1.6g (sat 0.4g)   Protein 23.6g
Carbohydrate 30.7g   Fiber 2.6g   Cholesterol 52mg   Sodium 471mg
Exchanges: 2 Starch, 3 Very Lean Meat

• • • • •

CARAMEL-BANANA SUNDAES

total time: 10 minutes

Combine ⅓ cup firmly packed brown sugar and 1 tablespoon water in a large nonstick skillet. Cook over medium heat until sugar melts. Add 2 large bananas, peeled and sliced, to skillet; cook over low heat 2 minutes or until banana is heated. Spoon banana mixture evenly over ½-cup portions of vanilla fat-free ice cream; top each serving with 1 teaspoon fat-free caramel topping.
Yield: 6 servings.

Per Serving: Calories 207 (1% from fat)   Fat 0.2g (sat 0.1g)   Protein 2.5g
Carbohydrate 49.0g   Fiber 1.3g   Cholesterol 0mg   Sodium 60mg
Exchanges: 2 Starch, 1 Fruit

An easy way to get a taste of New Orleans:
a gumbo-style soup, French bread, and Caramel-Banana Sundaes.

CHICKEN PEPPER POT

work time: 5 minutes • cook time: 4 hours or 8 hours

2   (16-ounce) packages frozen pepper stir-fry
4   (6-ounce) skinned chicken breast halves
1   (10¾-ounce) can low-fat, reduced-sodium tomato soup with
     garden herbs and peppercorns
1   tablespoon white wine Worcestershire sauce
½ teaspoon garlic salt

Place all ingredients in a 4- or 5-quart electric slow cooker. Cover
and cook on high setting 4 hours. Or, cover and cook on high setting
1 hour; reduce to low setting, and cook 7 hours.
Yield: 4 servings.

Per Serving: Calories 253 (13% from fat)   Fat 3.7g (sat 0.5g)   Protein 29.5g
Carbohydrate 25.2g   Fiber 4.9g   Cholesterol 66mg   Sodium 678mg
Exchanges: 1 Starch, 2 Vegetable, 3 Very Lean Meat

The savory chicken and peppers
are great over rice or noodles.

Add some French bread, and you've got a meal.

Grocery List

4 apples or pears

1 pound green beans

1½ pounds
sweet potatoes

4 whole wheat rolls

1 (14¼-ounce) can
fat-free, reduced-sodium
chicken broth

Apricot
spreadable fruit
(such as Polaner's)

Bay leaves

1 (1½-pound) package
turkey tenderloins

GLAZED TURKEY

work time: 3 minutes • cook time: 5 hours or 8 hours

4   sweet potatoes, scrubbed
1   turkey tenderloin (about ¾ pound)
1   (14¼-ounce) can fat-free, reduced-sodium chicken broth
2   bay leaves
½   cup apricot spreadable fruit

Place potatoes in bottom of a 5-quart electric slow cooker; place turkey over potatoes.
Pour broth over turkey; add bay leaves and spreadable fruit. Cover and cook on high setting 5 hours or until turkey is tender. Or, cover and cook on high setting 1 hour; reduce to low setting, and cook 7 hours. Remove and discard bay leaves. Slice and serve tenderloin with potatoes.
Yield: 4 servings.
Note: There are usually 2 tenderloins in a package; place the second one in an airtight container and freeze up to 1 month.

Per Serving: Calories 342 (5% from fat)   Fat 1.8g (sat 0.5g)   Protein 23.2g
Carbohydrate 56.6g   Fiber 5.1g   Cholesterol 51mg   Sodium 110mg
Exchanges: 4 Starch, 2 Very Lean Meat

Tender, glazed turkey and sweet potatoes—
a new twist for slow cooker fare.

Serve with green beans, wheat rolls, and fall apples.

Neapolitan Sundae, page 221

The number of ingredients Americans use in meal preparation is at an all-time low.

Mix & Match Recipes

Start with 5 ingredients. Combine creatively. Yield:

- green salads

- marinated vegetable salads

- beans, greens, and pasta salads

- strawberry desserts

- chocolate desserts

- raspberry desserts

- waffle desserts

Create a new salad for each weeknight meal with only 5 ingredients.

Grocery List

Red leaf lettuce (2 heads)

Cucumbers (5)

Plum tomatoes (11)

Reduced-fat olive oil vinaigrette (2 bottles)

Freshly ground pepper (optional)

Feta cheese (4-ounce package)

TOSSED SALAD

Combine 4 cups torn lettuce, ½ cucumber, chopped, 3 tomatoes, sliced, and ¼ cup vinaigrette; toss. Sprinkle each serving with 1 tablespoon crumbled feta cheese; sprinkle with freshly ground pepper, if desired.
Yield: 4 servings.

Per Serving: Calories 68 (63% from fat)   Fat 4.8g (sat 1.3g)   Protein 2.3g
Carbohydrate 5.3g   Fiber 1.6g   Cholesterol 6mg   Sodium 208mg
Exchanges: 1 Vegetable, 1 Fat

MARINATED CUCUMBERS AND TOMATOES

Combine 2 cucumbers, thinly sliced, 4 tomatoes, sliced and ½ cup vinaigrette. Cover and chill. Sprinkle with freshly ground pepper, if desired.

Yield: 4 servings.

Per Serving: Calories 73 (76% from fat)   Fat 6.2g (sat 0.5g)   Protein 0.5g
Carbohydrate 5.9g   Fiber 0.8g   Cholesterol 0mg   Sodium 246mg
Exchanges: 1 Vegetable, 1 Fat

MARINATED TOMATOES

Combine 4 tomatoes, sliced and ¼ cup vinaigrette. Cover and chill. Sprinkle each serving with 1 tablespoon crumbled feta cheese; sprinkle with freshly ground pepper, if desired.

Yield: 4 servings.

Per Serving: Calories 62 (68% from fat)   Fat 4.7g (sat 1.3g)   Protein 1.5g
Carbohydrate 4.7g   Fiber 0.8g   Cholesterol 6mg   Sodium 205mg
Exchanges: 1 Vegetable, 1 Fat

SIMPLY GREENS

Combine 8 cups torn lettuce and ¼ cup vinaigrette; toss. Sprinkle each serving with 1 tablespoon crumbled feta cheese; sprinkle with freshly ground pepper, if desired.

Yield: 4 (2-cup) servings.

Per Serving: Calories 67 (63% from fat)   Fat 4.7g (sat 1.3g)   Protein 2.8g
Carbohydrate 4.5g   Fiber 1.9g   Cholesterol 6mg   Sodium 208mg
Exchanges: 1 Vegetable, 1 Fat

MARINATED CUCUMBERS WITH FETA

Combine 2 cucumbers, thinly sliced and ¼ cup vinaigrette. Cover and chill. Sprinkle each serving with 1 tablespoon crumbled feta cheese; sprinkle with freshly ground pepper, if desired.

Yield: 4 servings.

Per Serving: Calories 49 (83% from fat)   Fat 4.5g (sat 1.3g)   Protein 1.0g
Carbohydrate 1.9g   Fiber 0.0g   Cholesterol 6mg   Sodium 199mg
Exchanges: ½ Vegetable, 1 Fat

Grocery List

Whole-kernel corn,
no-salt-added
(15.25-ounce cans)

Green beans,
no-salt-added
(14.5-ounce cans)

Lima beans
(15.25-ounce cans)

Kidney beans, no-salt-
added (15-ounce cans)

Sugar

Cider vinegar

Garlic powder

Vegetable seasoning
blend, frozen
(10-ounce package)

Make one batch of marinade,
and use it in a variety of salads—
all made from veggies in your pantry or freezer.

Corn Salad

Combine 2 (15.25-ounce) cans no-salt-added whole-kernel corn, drained, 1 package frozen vegetable seasoning blend, and ⅓ cup *Vegetable Salad Marinade* in a small bowl; stir well. Cover and marinate in refrigerator at least 4 hours, stirring occasionally. Serve with a slotted spoon.

Yield: 6 servings.

Per Serving: Calories 90 (9% from fat)   Fat 0.9g (sat 0.0g)   Protein 2.1g
Carbohydrate 19.1g   Fiber 1.2g   Cholesterol 0mg   Sodium 61mg
Exchanges: 1 Starch, 1 Vegetable

VEGETABLE SALAD MARINADE

Combine ⅔ cup sugar, 2 cups cider vinegar, 1 teaspoon salt, 1 teaspoon garlic powder, and 1 teaspoon pepper in a saucepan. Bring mixture to a boil, stirring constantly until sugar dissolves. Let cool. Cover; store in refrigerator up to 2 weeks. Stir before adding to vegetables.

Yield: 2⅓ cups.

Per ⅓ cup: Calories 85 (0% from fat)   Fat 0.0g (sat 0.0g)   Protein 0.1g
Carbohydrate 23.6g   Fiber 0.1g   Cholesterol 0mg   Sodium 336mg

GREEN BEAN SALAD

Combine 2 (14.5-ounce) cans no-salt-added green beans, drained, ½ package frozen vegetable seasoning blend, and ½ cup *Vegetable Salad Marinade* in a small bowl; stir well. Cover and marinate in refrigerator at least 4 hours, stirring occasionally. Serve with a slotted spoon.

Yield: 6 servings.

Per Serving: Calories 51 (4% from fat)   Fat 0.2g (sat 0.0g)   Protein 1.4g
Carbohydrate 12.5g   Fiber 1.8g   Cholesterol 0mg   Sodium 88mg
Exchange: 1 Starch

SUCCOTASH SALAD

Combine 1 (15.25-ounce) can no-salt-added whole-kernel corn, drained, 1 (15.25-ounce) can lima beans, drained, 1 package frozen vegetable seasoning blend, and ⅓ cup *Vegetable Salad Marinade* in a small bowl; stir well. Cover and marinate in refrigerator at least 4 hours, stirring occasionally. Serve with a slotted spoon.

Yield: 6 servings.

Per Serving: Calories 103 (6% from fat)   Fat 0.7g (sat 0.0g)   Protein 3.7g
Carbohydrate 21.3g   Fiber 1.8g   Cholesterol 0mg   Sodium 235mg
Exchanges: 1 Starch, 1 Vegetable

THREE-BEAN SALAD

Combine 1 (14.5-ounce) can no-salt-added green beans, drained, 1 (15.25-ounce) can lima beans, drained, 1 (15-ounce) can no-salt-added kidney beans, drained, ½ package frozen vegetable seasoning blend, and ½ cup *Vegetable Salad Marinade* in a bowl; stir. Cover and marinate in refrigerator at least 4 hours, stirring occasionally. Serve with a slotted spoon.

Yield: 6 servings.

Per Serving: Calories 137 (3% from fat)   Fat 0.4g (sat 0.1g)   Protein 7.1g
Carbohydrate 27.7g   Fiber 3.3g   Cholesterol 0mg   Sodium 352mg
Exchanges: 2 Starch

Create hearty salads with the Mediterranean trinity of beans, greens, and pastas.

GREEK PASTA SALAD

Combine 1 (15-ounce) can cannellini beans, drained and rinsed and 1 large tomato, chopped; stir well. Add 2 cups cooked penne pasta, ½ cup reduced-fat olive oil vinaigrette, and 2 cups finely shredded romaine lettuce, tossing to coat.

Yield: 6 (1-cup) servings.

Per Serving: Calories 148 (28% from fat)   Fat 4.6g (sat 0.4g)   Protein 4.8g
Carbohydrate 22.4g   Fiber 3.6g   Cholesterol 0mg   Sodium 374mg
Exchanges: 1 Starch, 1 Vegetable, 1 Fat

5 mix & match categories

Select one item from two or more of the five categories, and toss them together.

Canned Beans	Greens	Pasta	Dressings/Condiments	Fresh or Frozen Produce
Black†	Boston or Bibb	Fusilli	Balsamic Vinaigrette*	Corn (whole-kernel), frozen
Cannellini	Curly Leaf	Orzo	Caesar Italian Dressing*	Herbs
Garbanzo	Mixed Greens	Penne	Olive Oil Vinaigrette**	Onions (green and purple)
Kidney or Pinto†	Romaine	Tortellini	Roasted Garlic Italian Dressing*	Peppers (green, yellow, red)
Navy	Spinach	Ziti	Salsa	Tomatoes
†no-salt-added			*fat-free	
			**reduced-fat	

Spinach Tortellini with Kidney Beans

Cook and drain 4 ounces refrigerated spinach tortellini. Add 1 (15-ounce) can no-salt-added kidney beans, drained and rinsed, 2 tablespoons chopped green onions, and ½ cup fat-free roasted garlic Italian dressing, tossing lightly. Spoon mixture onto curly leaf lettuce leaves, if desired.

Yield: 4 (1-cup) servings.

Per Serving: Calories 204 (7% from fat)   Fat 1.6g (sat 0.7g)   Protein 10.2g
Carbohydrate 32.8g   Fiber 2.4g   Cholesterol 0mg   Sodium 476mg
Exchanges: 2 Starch, ½ Lean Meat

Tex-Mex Salad

Combine 1 (15-ounce) can no-salt-added black beans, drained and rinsed, ¼ cup chopped green onions, ¼ cup whole-kernel corn, thawed, and ½ cup salsa. Spoon bean mixture over 2 cups shredded romaine lettuce.

Yield: 4 servings.

Per Serving: Calories 111 (5% from fat)   Fat 0.6g (sat 0.1g)   Protein 6.9g
Carbohydrate 21.3g   Fiber 4.3g   Cholesterol 0mg   Sodium 103mg
Exchanges: 1 Starch, 1 Vegetable

Beans and Greens

Combine 1 (10-ounce) package mixed salad greens, 1 (16-ounce) can no-salt-added kidney beans, drained and rinsed, 1 (15-ounce) can cannellini beans, drained and rinsed, 1 medium-size purple onion, thinly sliced, and ½ cup reduced-fat olive oil vinaigrette.

Yield: 7 (1-cup) servings.

Per Serving: Calories 130 (26% from fat)   Fat 3.8g (sat 0.3g)   Protein 6.1g
Carbohydrate 18.7g   Fiber 4.4g   Cholesterol 0mg   Sodium 397mg
Exchanges: 1 Starch, 1 Vegetable, 1 Fat

White Bean and Tomato Salad

Combine 1 (15-ounce) can Navy beans, drained and rinsed, and 1 large tomato, chopped. Add ¼ cup fat-free balsamic vinaigrette, stirring to coat. Spoon bean mixture over Bibb lettuce leaves. Sprinkle with freshly ground pepper, if desired.

Yield: 4 servings.

Per Serving: Calories 78 (5% from fat)   Fat 0.4g (sat 0.0g)   Protein 3.7g
Carbohydrate 14.3g   Fiber 4.1g   Cholesterol 0mg   Sodium 350mg
Exchange: 1 Starch

Strawberries or chocolate ... or both.

2 basic ingredients plus 3 other items

equals 5 tempting desserts.

Grocery List

Strawberries, fresh or frozen, sliced, in light syrup (16 ounces)

Angel food cake
(1 loaf)

Reduced-fat chocolate chips (12-ounce bag)

Vanilla nonfat frozen yogurt (½ gallon)

Fat-free frozen whipped topping
(12-ounce container)

STRAWBERRY SHORTCAKES

Cut 4 (1-ounce) slices angel food cake, and place each slice on a plate. Top each slice with ½ cup sliced strawberries and ¼ cup whipped topping.

Yield: 4 servings.

Per Serving: Calories 125 (3% from fat)   Fat 0.4g (sat 0.0g)   Protein 2.2g   Carbohydrate 27.9g   Fiber 1.9g   Cholesterol 0mg   Sodium 155mg
Exchanges: 1 Starch, 1 Fruit

Neapolitan Sundaes

Place 1 cup sliced strawberries in container of an electric blender; cover and process until smooth.

Place ¼ cup chocolate chips in a small zip-top plastic bag, and crush with a meat mallet or rolling pin.

Cut 4 (1-ounce) slices angel food cake. Drizzle strawberry puree evenly on 4 plates, and place cake slices on top of puree. Top each with ⅓ cup frozen yogurt, and sprinkle each with 1 table-spoon crushed chocolate chips.

Yield: 4 servings.

Per Serving: Calories 193 (10% from fat) Fat 2.2g (sat 2.0g) Protein 4.5g
Carbohydrate 40.1g Fiber 0.9g Cholesterol 0mg Sodium 181mg
Exchanges: 2 Starch, ½ Fruit, ½ Fat

Chocolate Chip Frozen Yogurt

Fold ½ cup chocolate chips into 2 cups frozen yogurt. Spoon evenly into 4 dessert dishes.

Yield: 4 (½-cup) servings.

Per Serving: Calories 196 (18% from fat) Fat 4.0g (sat 4.0g) Protein 4.2g
Carbohydrate 36.7g Fiber 0.0g Cholesterol 0mg Sodium 56mg
Exchanges: 2½ Starch, 1 Fat

Strawberry Sundaes

Place 2 cups sliced strawberries in container of an electric blender. Cover and process until smooth. Spoon ½ cup frozen yogurt into each of 4 bowls. Spoon strawberry puree evenly over yogurt. Garnish with additional strawberry slices, if desired.

Yield: 4 servings.

Per Serving: Calories 98 (3% from fat) Fat 0.3g (sat 0.0g) Protein 3.6g
Carbohydrate 21.9g Fiber 1.9g Cholesterol 0mg Sodium 56mg
Exchanges: 1 Starch, ½ Fruit

Strawberry Whip Parfaits

Place 2 cups sliced strawberries in container of an electric blender. Cover and process until smooth, stopping once to scrape down sides. Fold strawberry puree into 2 cups fat-free whipped topping.

Cut 4 (1-ounce) slices angel food cake; tear into pieces, and fold into strawberry mixture. Spoon into parfait glasses; cover and chill.

Yield: 4 servings.

Per Serving: Calories 155 (2% from fat) Fat 0.4g (sat 0.0g) Protein 2.2g
Carbohydrate 33.9g Fiber 1.9g Cholesterol 0mg Sodium 165mg
Exchanges: 1 Starch, 1 Fruit

A chocolate-lover's dream.

Five ingredients — five luscious desserts.

Grocery List

Fresh raspberries (optional)

Fresh mint leaves (optional)

Raspberry fruit spread

Fat-free chocolate brownies (14-ounce package)

Chocolate wafer cookies (9-ounce package)

Reduced-fat chocolate frosting (16-ounce can)

Chocolate fat-free ice cream (½ gallon)

FROZEN CHOCOLATE BOMBE

Chill 1 (14-ounce) packaged brownie for 30 minutes. Cut brownie into pieces; pat pieces into a freezer-proof 1½-quart bowl lined with plastic wrap, forming a brownie bowl.

Stir 2 tablespoons fruit spread into 3 cups softened ice cream. Spoon into prepared brownie crust; cover and freeze 8 hours or until firm.

Melt ⅓ cup frosting in microwave at HIGH 45 seconds or until thin. Invert ice cream bombe onto a platter; coat with melted frosting. To serve, cut into 12 wedges. Spoon 2 tablespoons melted fruit spread onto each plate; top each serving with a wedge.

Yield: 12 servings.

Per Serving: Calories 231 (2% from fat)   Fat 0.6g (sat 0.2g)   Protein 3.0g
Carbohydrate 54.8g   Fiber 1.0g   Cholesterol 0mg   Sodium 171mg
Exchanges: 3 Starch, ½ Fruit

ICE CREAM SANDWICHES

For each sandwich, spread 3 tablespoons softened ice cream onto bottom of 1 wafer cookie, and top with a second wafer cookie. Wrap each sandwich in heavy-duty plastic wrap, and store in freezer.

Yield: 1 sandwich.

Per Sandwich: Calories 181 (34% from fat)   Fat 6.8g (sat 1.8g)   Protein 2.8g   Carbohydrate 27.3g   Fiber 0.0g   Cholesterol 26mg   Sodium 138mg
Exchanges: 2 Starch

BROWNIE SUNDAES

For each sundae, place 1 brownie (¹/₁₀ of package, cut into a triangle,) on a dessert plate. Serve with ⅓ cup ice cream, and drizzle with 1 tablespoon melted raspberry spread.

Yield: 1 serving.

Per Serving: Calories 205 (0% from fat)   Fat 0.0g (sat 0.0g)   Protein 3.4g   Carbohydrate 49.0g   Fiber 1.0g   Cholesterol 0mg   Sodium 173mg
Exchanges: 3 Starch

BROWNIE TORTE

Cut 1 (14-ounce) packaged brownie in half crosswise. Spread ¼ cup fruit spread on one half of brownie, and top with remaining brownie half. Melt ½ cup frosting in microwave at HIGH 45 seconds or until thin and smooth. Pour frosting over torte, spreading on top and sides of torte. To serve, slice crosswise into 8 pieces. Garnish with fresh raspberries and fresh mint leaves, if desired.

Yield: 8 servings.

Per Serving: 212 Calories (6% from fat)   Fat 1.3g (sat 0.5g)   Protein 2.8g   Carbohydrate 49.5g   Fiber 1.3g   Cholesterol 0mg   Sodium 188mg
Exchanges: 3 Starch

FROZEN CHOCOLATE PIE

Coat a 9-inch pieplate with cooking spray. Coarsely crush 8 chocolate wafer cookies; press crumbs into bottom of pieplate, and set aside. Slightly soften 3 cups ice cream in microwave, and spoon over prepared crumbs. Top ice cream with 5 additional crushed wafer cookies; cover and freeze 2 hours or until firm. To serve, cut into wedges.

Yield: 8 servings.

Per Serving: Calories 214 (24% from fat)   Fat 5.6g (sat 1.5g)   Protein 3.2g   Carbohydrate 37.3g   Fiber 0.0g   Cholesterol 21mg   Sodium 142mg
Exchanges: 2½ Starch

Raspberries,
fresh or frozen

Fat-free pound cake loaf

Vanilla fat-free pudding
(1 snack pack of four
3.5-ounce cartons)

Lemon low-fat yogurt
(8-ounce cartons)

Fat-free frozen
whipped topping
(12-ounce container)

Five rave-worthy,
no-cook raspberry desserts

Combine fresh or frozen berries with ingredients
you have on hand.

RASPBERRY TRIFLE

Cut one-half loaf fat-free pound cake into cubes; place cubes on bottom
of a 2-quart glass bowl or trifle dish. Top with 3 (3.5-ounce) cartons
vanilla fat-free pudding and 1½ cups raspberries.

Yield: 6 servings.

Per Serving: Calories 152 (1% from fat)   Fat 0.2g (sat 0.0g)   Protein 2.6g
Carbohydrate 31.2g   Fiber 2.6g   Cholesterol 0mg   Sodium 202mg
Exchanges: 1 Starch, 1 Fruit

RASPBERRY SMOOTHIES

Combine 1 (8-ounce) carton lemon low-fat yogurt, 1½ cups whipped topping, 1½ cups raspberries, and 5 ice cubes in container of an electric blender; cover and process until smooth.
Yield: 4 (1-cup) servings.

Per Serving: Calories 144 (4% from fat)   Fat 0.7g (sat 0.0g)   Protein 2.5g
Carbohydrate 30.8g   Fiber 3.1g   Cholesterol 0mg   Sodium 52mg
Exchanges: 1 Starch, 1 Fruit

RASPBERRY SHORTCAKES

Slice one-half loaf fat-free pound cake into 4 slices; cut each slice into 2 triangles, and place evenly on plates. Top each serving with ½ cup raspberries and 1 tablespoon whipped topping.
Yield: 4 servings.

Per Serving: Calories 168 (2% from fat)   Fat 0.3g (sat 0.0g)   Protein 2.6g
Carbohydrate 36.6g   Fiber 5.1g   Cholesterol 0mg   Sodium 193mg
Exchanges: 1½ Starch, 1 Fruit

FROZEN RASPBERRY DESSERTS

Line 8 muffin cups with paper muffin liners. Fold together 2 (3.5-ounce) cartons vanilla fat-free pudding, 1 cup whipped topping, and ½ cup raspberries. Divide mixture evenly among muffin cups; cover and freeze at least 2 hours.
Yield: 8 servings.

Per Serving: Calories 39 (0% from fat)   Fat 0.0g (sat 0.0g)   Protein 0.6g
Carbohydrate 8.4g   Fiber 0.6g   Cholesterol 0mg   Sodium 43mg
Exchange: ½ Fruit

RASPBERRY-LEMON PARFAITS

Layer 2 cups raspberries and 2 (8-ounce) cartons lemon low-fat yogurt evenly into 4 (6-ounce) parfait glasses, beginning and ending with raspberries.
Yield: 4 servings.

Per Serving: Calories 183 (6% from fat)   Fat 1.2g (sat 0.0g)   Protein 4.8g
Carbohydrate 40.0g   Fiber 4.2g   Cholesterol 0mg   Sodium 74mg
Exchanges: 1½ Starch, 1 Fruit

Transform frozen breakfast waffles

into wonderful desserts with combinations of only 4 more ingredients.

Grocery List

Strawberries, fresh or frozen, sliced, in light syrup (16 ounces)

Canned crushed pineapple (8-ounce cans)

Fat-free chocolate sauce (1 jar)

Sugar

Cinnamon

Reduced-fat frozen waffles (11-ounce package)

Vanilla nonfat frozen yogurt (½ gallon)

STRAWBERRY-WAFFLE SHORTCAKES

Spoon ½ cup sliced strawberries over each of 4 toasted waffles; top each with 2 tablespoons slightly softened frozen yogurt.

Yield: 4 servings.

Per Serving: Calories 132 (10% from fat)   Fat 1.5g (sat 0.3g)   Protein 4.3g
Carbohydrate 27.0g   Fiber 2.3g   Cholesterol 13mg   Sodium 175mg
Exchanges: 1 Starch, 1 Fruit

LAYERED WAFFLE-FRUIT CUP

Toast 4 waffles, and tear into small pieces.

Combine 1 cup chopped strawberries, ½ cup canned crushed pineapple, drained, and 1 cup frozen yogurt.

Divide half of waffle pieces among 4 parfait glasses. Spoon ⅓ cup yogurt mixture over waffle pieces in each glass. Repeat procedure with remaining half of waffle pieces and yogurt mixture.

Yield: 4 servings.

Per Serving: Calories 149 (9% from fat)   Fat 1.5g (sat 0.3g)   Protein 4.9g
Carbohydrate 30.9g   Fiber 1.6g   Cholesterol 13mg   Sodium 189mg
Exchanges: 1 Starch, 1 Fruit

WAFFLEWICHES

Toast 4 waffles. Spread ½ cup softened frozen yogurt over each of 2 toasted waffles. Top with remaining 2 toasted waffles.

Cut each wafflewich into 4 wedges, and drizzle 2 tablespoons chocolate sauce evenly over wedges.

Yield: 4 servings (serving size: 2 wedges).

Per Serving: Calories 152 (8% from fat)   Fat 1.4g (sat 0.3g)   Protein 4.9g
Carbohydrate 31.4g   Fiber 0.5g   Cholesterol 13mg   Sodium 194mg
Exchanges: 2 Starch

FRUITED FROZEN YOGURT

Stir 1 (8-ounce) can crushed pineapple, drained (or ½ cup chopped strawberries) into 2 cups slightly softened frozen yogurt. Serve with Cinnamon Waffle Crisps, if desired.

Yield: 4 (½-cup) servings.

Per Serving: Calories 98 (0% from fat)   Fat 0.0g (sat 0.0g)   Protein 3.3g
Carbohydrate 22.5g   Fiber 0.3g   Cholesterol 0mg   Sodium 56mg
Exchanges: ½ Starch, 1 Fruit

CINNAMON WAFFLE CRISPS

Combine 1 tablespoon sugar and ¼ teaspoon ground cinnamon, stirring well.

Coat 2 frozen waffles with butter-flavored cooking spray, and sprinkle each with ½ tablespoon sugar mixture. Place on a baking sheet; bake at 450° for 5 to 7 minutes or until crisp. Cut each waffle into 4 wedges. Serve with frozen yogurt, if desired.

Yield: 4 servings (serving size: 2 wedges).

Per Serving: Calories 59 (12% from fat)   Fat 0.8g (sat 0.1g)   Protein 1.5g
Carbohydrate 12.0g   Fiber 0.3g   Cholesterol 6mg   Sodium 80mg
Exchange: 1 Starch

Nutrition Notes

The recipes and meals in the *5-Ingredient 15-Minute Cookbook* help you meet the healthy eating recommendations of the U.S. Dietary Guidelines. Use the nutrient analysis following each recipe to see how the recipe fits into your healthy eating plan.

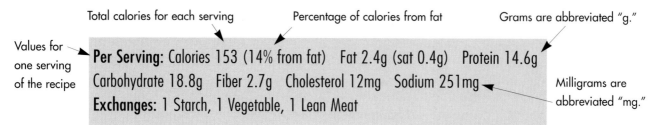

Total calories for each serving

Percentage of calories from fat

Grams are abbreviated "g."

Values for one serving of the recipe

Per Serving: Calories 153 (14% from fat) Fat 2.4g (sat 0.4g) Protein 14.6g
Carbohydrate 18.8g Fiber 2.7g Cholesterol 12mg Sodium 251mg
Exchanges: 1 Starch, 1 Vegetable, 1 Lean Meat

Milligrams are abbreviated "mg."

FAT

Your daily fat intake should be 30 percent or less of your total calories for the day. This doesn't mean that every single food you eat has to be under 30 percent.

Recipes with over 30 percent calories from fat can still be healthy. For example, salmon is higher in fat than other fish, but it is omega-3 fat, a healthier kind of fat. And for recipes with very low-calorie foods like vegetables, the total amount of fat can be low but still make up a large percentage of the calories.

Here's how the 30 percent recommendation translates to actual fat grams per day:

If you should eat 2000 calories per day, you can have up to 67 grams of fat:
2000 calories x 30% = 600 calories
600 calories ÷ 9 calories per gram = 67 grams fat

SODIUM

The current dietary recommendations advise us to limit our sodium to 2,400 milligrams a day. As you enjoy the ease of using convenience products, be aware that many of them are high in sodium, even when they are low in fat and calories. If you're watching your sodium intake carefully, read food labels and note the sodium value in the nutrient analysis following each recipe. We use reduced-sodium products as often as possible in these recipes to keep sodium to a minimum.

DIABETIC EXCHANGES

Exchange values are provided for people who use them for meal planning. The values are based on the *Exchange Lists for Meal Planning* developed by the American Diabetes Association and The American Dietetic Association.

DAILY NUTRITION GUIDE

Use the values from the U.S. Dietary Guidelines in the chart below to determine your daily nutrient needs.

	women ages 25 to 50	*women over 50*	*men over 24*
Calories*	2,000	2,000 or less	2,700
Protein	50g	50g or less	63g
Fat	67g or less	67g or less	90g or less
Saturated Fat	22g or less	22g or less	30g or less
Carbohydrate	299g	299g	405g
Fiber	25g to 35g	25g to 35g	25g to 35g
Cholesterol	300mg or less	300mg or less	300mg or less
Sodium	2,400mg or less	2,400mg or less	2,400mg or less

*Calorie requirements vary according to your size, weight, and level of activity. The calorie level in the chart is a general guide; you may need more calories if you are pregnant, breastfeeding, or trying to gain weight, or less if you are trying to lose or maintain weight.

Microwave Cooking Chart

Cooking vegetables in the microwave is the best way to preserve nutrients and flavor, and often the quickest way to cook them. Cook all the vegetables at HIGH power in a baking dish covered with wax paper. If you use plastic wrap to cover the dish, be sure to turn back one corner to allow steam to escape.

Food	Microwave Cooking Time	Special Instructions
Asparagus, 1 pound	6 to 7 minutes	Add ¼ cup water
Beans, green, 1 pound	14 to 15 minutes	Add ½ cup water
Broccoli spears, 1 pound	7 to 8 minutes	Arrange in a circle, spoke-fashion, with flowerets in center; add ½ cup water
Carrot slices, 1 pound	9 to 10 minutes; stand 2 minutes	Add ¼ cup water
Cauliflower flowerets, 1 pound	7 to 8 minutes; stand 2 minutes	Add ¼ cup water
Corn on the cob, 2 (large) ears 3 ears 4 ears	5 to 9 minutes 7 to 12 minutes 8 to 15 minutes	Arrange end-to-end in a circle; add ¼ cup water
Onions, 1 pound, peeled and quartered	6 to 8 minutes	Add 2 tablespoons water
Peas, green, shelled, 1 pound (about 1½ cups)	6 to 7 minutes	Add 2 tablespoons water
Potatoes, baking/sweet, medium 1 potato 2 potatoes 4 potatoes	4 to 6 minutes 7 to 8 minutes 12 to 14 minutes	Pierce skins and arrange end-to-end in a circle; let stand 5 minutes after cooking
New potatoes, 1 pound	8 to 10 minutes	Pierce if unpeeled; add ¼ cup water
Spinach, 10-ounce package fresh leaves	2 to 3 minutes	Wash leaves before cooking
Squash, Yellow/Zucchini, 1 pound, sliced (4 medium)	7 to 8 minutes	Add ¼ cup water
Squash, Acorn, 2 pounds, (2 medium)	9 to 10 minutes	Pierce skins
Turnips, 1¼ pounds, peeled and cubed (4 medium)	10 to 12 minutes	Add ¼ cup water

Metric Equivalents

The recipes that appear in this cookbook use the standard United States method for measuring liquid and dry or solid ingredients (teaspoons, tablespoons, and cups). The information in the following charts is provided to help cooks outside the U.S. successfully use these recipes. All equivalents are approximate.

Equivalents for Different Types of Ingredients

A standard cup measure of a dry or solid ingredient will vary in weight depending on the type of ingredient.

A standard cup of liquid is the same volume for any type of liquid. Use the following chart when converting standard cup measures to grams (weight) or milliliters (volume).

Standard Cup	Fine Powder (ex. flour)	Grain (ex. rice)	Granular (ex. sugar)	Liquid Solids (ex. butter)	Liquid (ex. milk)
1	140 g	150 g	190 g	200 g	240 ml
¾	105 g	113 g	143 g	150 g	180 ml
⅔	93 g	100 g	125 g	133 g	160 ml
½	70 g	75 g	95 g	100 g	120 ml
⅓	47 g	50 g	63 g	67 g	80 ml
¼	35 g	38 g	48 g	50 g	60 ml
⅛	18 g	19 g	24 g	25 g	30 ml

Dry Ingredients by Weight

(To convert ounces to grams, multiply the number of ounces by 30.)

1 oz	=	¹⁄₁₆ lb	=	30 g
4 oz	=	¼ lb	=	120 g
8 oz	=	½ lb	=	240 g
12 oz	=	¾ lb	=	360 g
16 oz	=	1 lb	=	480 g

Length

(To convert inches to centimeters, multiply the number of inches by 2.5.)

1 in			=	2.5 cm		
6 in	=	½ ft	=	15 cm		
12 in	=	1 ft	=	30 cm		
36 in	=	3 ft	= 1 yd	=	90 cm		
40 in			=	100 cm	=	1 meter

Liquid Ingredients by Volume

¼ tsp							1 ml
½ tsp							2 ml
1 tsp							5 ml
3 tsp	=	1 tbls			=	½ fl oz	=	15 ml
		2 tbls	=	⅛ cup	=	1 fl oz	=	30 ml
		4 tbls	=	¼ cup	=	2 fl oz	=	60 ml
		5⅓ tbls	=	⅓ cup	=	3 fl oz	=	80 ml
		8 tbls	=	½ cup	=	4 fl oz	=	120 ml
		10⅔ tbls	=	⅔ cup	=	5 fl oz	=	160 ml
		12 tbls	=	¾ cup	=	6 fl oz	=	180 ml
		16 tbls	=	1 cup	=	8 fl oz	=	240 ml
		1 pt	=	2 cups	=	16 fl oz	=	480 ml
		1 qt	=	4 cups	=	32 fl oz	=	960 ml
						33 fl oz	=	1000 ml = 1 liter

Cooking/Oven Temperatures

	Fahrenheit	Celsius	Gas Mark
Freeze Water	32° F	0° C	
Room Temperature	68° F	20° C	
Boil Water	212° F	100° C	
Bake	325° F	160° C	3
	350° F	180° C	4
	375° F	190° C	5
	400° F	200° C	6
	425° F	220° C	7
	450° F	230° C	8
Broil			Grill

Recipe Index

See page 239 for lists of Side Dish Recipes.

Side Dish Recipes

If you want to create your own meal combinations with the recipes in this book, use these lists to find the perfect side dish for your entrée.

Grains and Pastas

Couscous, Broccoli, 147
Couscous with Walnuts, Curried, 138
Noodles, Asian, 134
Rice, Curried, 119
Rice, Orange, 149
Rice, Saffron, 25

Salads

Apple Salad, Tossed, 69
Bean and Tomato Salad, White, 219
Bean-Rice Salad, Black, 21
Bean Salad, Green, 217
Bean Salad, Three-, 217
Beans and Greens, 219
Bok Choy and Tomato Salad, 186
Cantaloupe with Raspberry-Poppy Seed
   Dressing, 129
Coleslaw, Zesty, 15
Corn Salad, 216
Corn Salad, Mexican, 183
Cranberry Waldorf Salad, 116
Cucumbers and Tomatoes, Marinated, 215
Cucumbers with Feta, Marinated, 215
Greens, Simply, 215
Italian-Style Salad, 198
Melon Duo, Refreshing, 142
Melon Salad, Gingered, 156
Pasta Salad, Greek, 218
Radish-Cauliflower Salad, Crunchy, 72
Romaine Salad, 77

Slaw, Honey-Kissed, 176
Slaw, Quick Veggie, 200
Spinach-Onion Salad, 40
Spinach Salad, Sweet-and-Sour, 137
Succotash Salad, 217
Tex-Mex Salad, 219
Tomatoes, Marinated, 215
Tomato Salad, Balsamic, 189
Tortellini with Kidney Beans, Spinach, 219
Tossed Salad, 214

Vegetables

Asparagus Packets, Lemon-, 29
Asparagus, Roasted, 112
Beans and Tomatoes, Skillet, 109
Beans, Green Chile Refried, 185
Beans in a Pot, Baked, 179
Carrots, Lemon, 102
Corn on the Cob, Dilled, 40
Peas, Herbed Sugar Snap, 145
Peas, Steamed Snow, 26
Pepper, Sautéed Green, 160
Potatoes, Baked, 98
Potatoes, Brown Sugar Sweet, 120
Potatoes, Garlic Mashed, 94
Potatoes, Steamed, 115
Squash Medley, Summer, 105
Vegetable Crudités, 190
Zucchini, Skillet, 31
Zucchini Sticks, 34

. . . . .

Acknowledgments

OXMOOR HOUSE WISHES TO THANK THE FOLLOWING MERCHANTS:

Aletha Soulé, The Loom Co., New York, NY

Annieglass, Watsonville, CA

Barbara Eigen Arts, Inc., Jersey City, NJ

Big Sky Bakery, Birmingham, AL

Biot, New York, NY

Carolyn Rice Art Pottery, Marietta, GA

Cyclamen Studio, Inc., Berkeley, CA

Edgar's, Birmingham, AL

E & M Glass, Cheshire, UK

Fioriware, Zanesville, OH

Judy Jackson Pottery, New York, NY

Marge Margulies Pottery, Philadelphia, PA

Mariposa, Manchester, MA

Over and Back, Ronkonkoma, NY

Pastis and Company, New York, NY

Potluck, Accord, NY

Sabre Flatware, Paris, France

Smyer Glass, Benicia, CA

Union Glass, San Francisco, CA

V. Richards, Birmingham, AL

Vietri, Hillsborough, NC

. . . . .

Source of Nutrient Analysis Data: Computrition, Inc.,
Chatsworth, CA, and information provided by food manufacturers

. . . . .